BIRDS OF PREY

BIRDS OF PREY

Floyd Scholz

Photographs by Tad Merrick

STACKPOLE
BOOKS

Published by
STACKPOLE BOOKS
5067 Ritter Road
Mechanicsburg, PA 17055

Photographs by Tad Merrick (unless otherwise credited)
Species profile drawings by Floyd Scholz
Species head portraits by Reed A. Prescott III
Wing line drawings by Barry Van Dusen
Interior design by Tracy Patterson
Interior layout by Marcia Lee Dobbs

Printed in Hong Kong

10 9 8 7 6 5 4 3 2

First Edition

Library of Congress Cataloging-in-Publication Data

Scholz, Floyd.
    Birds of prey / Floyd Scholz ; photographs by Tad Merrick. —
1st ed.
        p.   cm.
    ISBN 0-8117-0242-1
    1. Birds of prey—North America.   I. Title.
QL696.F3S33   1993
598'.91'097—dc20   93-12426
                                                            CIP

Dedicated to Floyd L. Scholz, Sr.,
my father, my mentor, my friend

In memoriam to
George Csefai
and
John Scheeler

CONTENTS

ACKNOWLEDGMENTS

THERE ARE MANY PEOPLE TO WHOM I AM DEEPLY indebted and to whom I wish to express my heartfelt gratitude. Without their support, encouragement, and incredible patience, this book would never have been possible.

First and foremost, to my wife, Beatriz—without her love and understanding, this book would never have been possible (it's not easy being married to an artist). To my mother, Muriel, who taught me more about life and our natural world than she'll ever know; my stepchildren, Ramon, Helenia, Beatriz, and Elizabeth, who are truly the best of the best; Dr. Myron Yanoff, Dr. Karin Yanoff, and Alexis Yanoff; my aunt Donna Bejak; a mi familia Venezolana por aceptarme en sus vidas; Eldridge Arnold; Larry Barth; Greg Woodard; Frank Fekete; Ernie Muehlmatt; Dick and Dorothy Robson; Mike and Julia Kinsley; my good friend and cohort on this book, Tad Merrick, and his wife, Janice; the staff at V.I.N.S., especially Julie Tracy and Nancy Reed; Jack Oliver; Reed Prescott III; Barry Van Dusen; Cindy Kilgore Brown; Diane and the Vermont home bakery; Ben and Anna Bailar; and my fellow carver and friend Gary Denzler. A huge thank you to Jamie Dailley, Carole Precious, Brian Fleming, and the wonderful staff of African Lion Safari in Ontario, Canada. To Bob and Leslie Novack; Brian Cole; Diane White; my friends Simon Perkins, Wayne Peterson, and the staff of the Massachusetts Audubon chapter; Claire Walker Leslie, my comrade in arms; and my fellow raptor fanatics and falconers extraordinaire of the Long Island Falconers Association, Jim Bonelli, Ted Diamont, Sam Nahman, Brian Hyland, Marc Marrone, Robert Harrison, and their fabulous birds. Many thanks to my good buddy Peter Capainolo and Jesibelle; James Zingo; Peter Schmidt for allowing us access to photograph some great birds; Paul and Meta Doherty; Joe Simeone and Dick Zibner; Roger Schroeder, who really got the ball rolling; Jack Murray; Ernie Simmons; Rob Braunfield; fellow carver and great artist Gloria Young; Roger Jones; and the late, great John Scheeler.

Last, but most certainly not least, thanks to my editor, Judith Schnell, to David Uhler and the staff at Stackpole Books, and to Cathy Hart and the staff of *Wildfowl Carving and Collecting* magazine. My apologies go to anyone I may have inadvertently neglected to mention. Thank you all so very much!

Floyd Scholz
Hancock, Vermont

FOREWORD

ALL ARTISTS RELY ON SOME SORT OF SOURCE MATERIAL. Whether one is an imaginative painter working from past memories or a meticulous renderer detailing every strand of hair, some kind of reference is necessary.

I am a painter whose favorite subjects are mammals and birds, and whose favorite birds are the birds of prey. I wince when I think of what I had to go through to obtain good reference material when I began painting. Acquiring such material in this demanding and competitive field is particularly difficult when one is first starting out. For anyone who works with these winged hunters, whether in two or three dimensions, whether beginner or veteran, the contents of this book are a dream come true. It has the most complete visual reference material ever published on seventeen of the major North American diurnal birds of prey. For the artist the text is just as thorough, with explanations of such details as eye ridges, beak shapes, talon variations, and so forth. For the carver there is a step-by-step painting of a kestrel.

Floyd Scholz brings the same thoroughness and excellence to *Birds of Prey* that is so evident in his meticulous carvings featured at the end of the book. How fortunate we all are to benefit from his efforts. This is a book to be appreciated by anyone the least bit interested in the birds of prey, and one that is long overdue.

Guy Coheleach
Bernardsville, New Jersey

INTRODUCTION

WE HEARD IT BEFORE WE SAW IT. THE CRY OF A FAR-off blue jay was the only indicator of the drama that was about to unfold. A sharp whistle of wind tore directly over our heads, followed by an even louder sound like ripping canvas.

My feet felt anchored to the ledge as we watched the rock dove twisting and turning, plummeting into the valley below in an attempt to evade its determined pursuer. Despite impressive speed and mastery of flight, the dove's every move was mirrored as the distance between hunter and hunted decreased. Banking sharply to the left, the dove momentarily added to the span of sky that separated the two. But with the flick of a wing tip the hungry falcon was back on track and bearing down. Suddenly, with an explosion of feathers, the deadly game was over. This time the falcon came away the victor; more often than not, it won't.

Lasting no more than eight seconds, this scene will be with me forever. This predatory success had special meaning for those present that late July afternoon on Mount Horrid in Vermont's Green National Forest. One of the fledgling peregrine falcons so carefully tended over the past six weeks by the staff of the Peregrine Fund had scored its first kill.

I can't remember a time in my life when I wasn't thrilled and fascinated by birds of prey. With their sharply hooked beaks, daggerlike talons, and piercing eyes, these powerful winged hunters patrol the heavens in search of their next victim. What young imaginative mind could possibly resist such creatures?

I often tagged along with my father during his many hunting trips, listening to and marveling at the many stories that he and my uncle would tell of the secrets concealed within the fields, streams, and forests. Bagging a buck or returning home with pheasant or grouse seemed unimportant. To be out in the woods away from honking horns, traffic lights, and crowds was my idea of what life should be.

Often on an autumn day I would go off to play in the woods. Hiding in the brush, climbing high into the trees, I pretended to be a predator. I was the feared king of the woods lying in wait for some unsuspecting animal to wander by, but of course, none ever did. What I did see were hawks, lots of hawks soaring overhead scanning the fields for mice and rabbits. And I wondered how it must feel to be truly free to ride the winds. The more I watched, the more I wanted to learn about these elusive hunters of the sky.

I was eight years old when my uncle George Csefai, a Hungarian immigrant, began carving decoys to supplement his hunting rigs. A machinist by trade, Uncle George was one of those people blessed with a sharp eye, a creative mind, and highly skilled hands; not surprisingly, he took to carving and got very good very fast. My parents and I accompanied him to the 1971 U.S. National Decoy Show where he won many top honors in the amateur class. As far as I was concerned these carver-artists were magicians transforming ordinary blocks of wood into living, breathing birds. After that weekend, my uncle's workshop took on

CINDY KILGORE-BROWN

A peregrine falcon banks sharply over the Green Mountains of Vermont in pursuit of its feathered quarry.

new meaning. Although I was intrigued by the many ducks and shorebirds that left his studio, it was his carved hawks that really excited me. In mid 1972 he was beginning work on a bald eagle when he became very ill; six months later he died. I was crushed. I had already begun carving a few birds of my own, and realizing my interest in my uncle's

artwork my father and my aunt saw to it that many of his carving tools and books were given to me. My fledgling hobby was now gaining momentum.

Like many novice bird carvers, I began carving ducks. For the first five years I worked on the rudimentary techniques, still not feeling confident enough to tackle my real favorites, the magnificent birds of prey. In 1977 I decided to give it a try and carved a three-quarter-size red-tailed hawk. I was hooked. Kestrels followed, as did screech owls, more kestrels, and merlins. I couldn't wait to get started on the next one. All this time I relied on pictures from field guides, encyclopedias, and books I borrowed from the local Audubon Society. Little did I know that I was setting myself up for the biggest shock of my life. Although I had many pictures available for references, along with some vague field guide measurements, I had never actually seen a live raptor up close.

In late 1978 I had just finished painting an American kestrel of which I was really proud—so proud in fact that I took it up to the local Audubon Society to show it off to my friends. That same weekend someone had brought by an injured kestrel. As I was taking my carving out of the box, they brought over the little chattering male kestrel. When I saw them side by side, I wanted to climb into the box and die. My carving was grossly oversize, the eyes were wrong, the coloring was off, and I had omitted many major plumage details! Two weeks passed before I could summon up the courage to sit back at my workbench and try again.

I learned a valuable lesson that day: you can't carve what you don't know. To this day I emphasize that time studying the living bird is time well spent.

This philosophy has taken me many wonderful places shared with many different people. A desire to carve a peregrine falcon led me to Cornell University's hawk barns and involvement with the Peregrine Fund. To learn more about puffins I volunteered to work with Dr. Steve Kress's puffin project and spent many glorious days on the islands off the coast of Maine. I've noticed that as an artist I tend to look at birds differently from many of my ornithological friends. This book is the result of my frustration at the lack of good, clear visual information on birds of prey. Over the last twelve years of working as a professional artist, I've realized that although much has been written on the scientific characteristics of North American raptors, nothing was available for the average person who just wanted to know more about what these marvelous birds look like up close.

Consider this book a celebration—a celebration of these birds for their elegance and beauty.

What Is a Raptor?

THROUGHOUT RECORDED HISTORY, BIRDS OF PREY have played a major role as civilizations developed. They seem to symbolize many of the qualities to which humans aspire. Strong, fearless, powerful, and independent are some of the many terms that have been used to describe this magnificent group of birds. It is easy to see why. Not only do they possess the armaments to quickly overcome and kill their prey, but they also can do something that until very recently humans could only dream of doing: they can fly.

The term "raptor" is derived from the Latin *raptor* meaning plunderer (from the verb to snatch, seize).

Raptors fall into two categories: diurnal raptors (daytime predators) and nocturnal raptors (nighttime predators). The group of diurnal raptors is made up of falcons, hawks, eagles, ospreys, old- and new-world vultures, and the secretary birds of Africa; collectively all these are known as the order Falconiformes. The group of nocturnal raptors is made up of owls (order Strigiformes).

This book is by no means intended to be an ornithological text on raptors. My goal is to provide an illustrated volume focusing on the visible physical characteristics of some of the more common North American diurnal birds of prey—an artist's reference guide that can offer valuable information to anyone interested in learning more about what these elusive birds really look like. Fortunately, birds of prey are now federally protected. This law, although beneficial to the birds, makes it impossible for the average person to get "up close and personal" with a hawk or an owl. Waterfowl can readily be purchased and kept in a backyard aviary for observation, but to get a good opportunity to really see and photograph raptors, you must either have access to a raptor rehabilitation center or get to know a falconer.

Most raptors must kill other animals in order to survive. The faster the raptor can kill its prey, the less chance it has of being injured in the process. Some of the physical characteristics that birds of prey have developed for survival are described below.

Eyes

Most birds of prey rely heavily on sight to locate their food. For this they have evolved large, extremely sensitive eyes. If you ever have an opportu-

This close-up head profile of a golden eagle shows the eye-to-bill relationship and the flattened, sloping top of the head.

This photo of an adult light-phase ferruginous hawk highlights the true binocular vision and the pronounced gape of the beak.

A close-up of the head profile and chest of a light-phase ferruginous hawk.

Note the large eye and the bony tubercle in the nostril of this tiercel (male) peregrine falcon.

CINDY KILGORE-BROWN

Full vision is unobstructed on this Harris' hawk, even from below. This is probably an adaptation for scanning the ground from high above.

Close-up of a relaxed male Harris' hawk. Note the nearly bare-skinned lore area in front of the eyes.

This falcon's nostril is specially designed to allow it to breathe during its spectacular high-speed dives. It was once thought that the larger and more complex the bony tubercle was, the faster the bird could fly, but this theory has never been proven.

nity to look closely at a hawk's eye, you will notice that it can focus incredibly fast. The pupil can adjust its size in milliseconds, and the eye possesses a bulbous lens, or cornea.

In the entire bird world, birds of prey probably have the most acute eyesight. Based on the physical structure of a hawk's eye, scientists believe that the eyes of some raptors are up to eight times more acute than those of humans. Such sensitive equipment needs to be carefully protected. For an artist, one of the appealing physical characteristics of diurnal raptors, in my opinion, is the heavy-browed "tough guy" look. This heavy ridge or eyebrow is thought to offer two advantages: it provides shade for the supersensitive eyes and it deflects dust, debris, and other foreign particles while the hawk is engaged in high-speed pursuit of its prey. Artistically, the brow and eye of most diurnal raptors is one of the areas that must be rendered with extreme accuracy if you hope to do a convincing sculpture or painting. Take time to notice the subtleties in the head structures of different hawks, falcons, and eagles. I cannot stress enough how important it is to concentrate on the head and face of the subject, because it is this small area that can convey the essence of the species you are striving to portray.

Bills

The most imposing part of a raptor's head has to be the bill. Stout, thick, and sharply hooked, it is a highly specialized tool. Each bird of prey has some modifications of its bill in accordance with its specific dietary needs. This fact is especially obvious with the snail kite, whose upper mandible has a long, narrow hook that allows it to feed on apple snails. With careful study of a raptor's bill structure you can accurately conclude what prey items make up a large part of its diet. Falcons, for instance, have developed a "tooth" on the ridge of their upper mandible. Called a tomial tooth, it is designed to lock onto and efficiently sever the neck bones of smaller birds.

The soft, fleshy part of the bill is called the cere. The nostrils are located here. Notice that falcons have a bony baffle in the nostril. It is thought that this baffle allows the falcon to breathe during its extremely high-speed dives.

A bird's bill is made of a material called keratin, and as the bill grows it continually sheds and flakes off, especially near the tip and edges. It is much like your fingernail in structure and feel, and on close inspection you will notice very subtle growth ridges following the direction of growth from the cere to the sharp tip.

Be very careful when obtaining bill measurements from a study skin or mounted bird, as this area shrinks considerably once the bird dies.

Feet

A commonly held theory currently is that birds are highly evolved dinosaurs—that a bird's feathers are just evolved reptilian scales and that dinosaurs were warm-blooded creatures. Take a look at the feet of any raptor and the dinosaur theory seems quite likely. Heavily scaled and very reptilian looking, they are the raptor's first line of defense and food acquisition. On close inspection you will notice that the length of the toes varies considerably, as do the length and thickness of the talons. On most raptors the largest and thickest talon is on the rear toe (which is called the hallux), the smallest on the outer toe.

The majority of the killing and grasping power of the foot resides in the rear and inside talons. Understandably these two toes are the thickest and shortest, allowing for much greater leverage and power. These toes also have one less joint than do the middle and outside toes.

The feet are highly specialized according to species. The falcons and accipiters, whose diets consist largely of birds (an extremely mobile and evasive prey), have long, slender toes and a longer leg (or tarsus), giving them a larger area to grasp with. Ospreys have specialized pads with little spines called spicules that enable them to grab and hold onto slippery fish. They also possess the ability to swivel their outside toe to the rear, which enables them to carry heavier prey items. Moreover, the osprey has the distinction of being the only North American hawklike bird that has totally round talons. All other raptors' talons are either flat or slightly concave along the bottom (a subtle but important detail when rendering accurate feet).

The outer toe is connected to the middle toe with a broad web of skin on most raptor species in North America.

This is the part of a golden eagle that small animals' nightmares are made of. The inside talon (pictured) and rear talon can attain lengths of up to 3 inches!

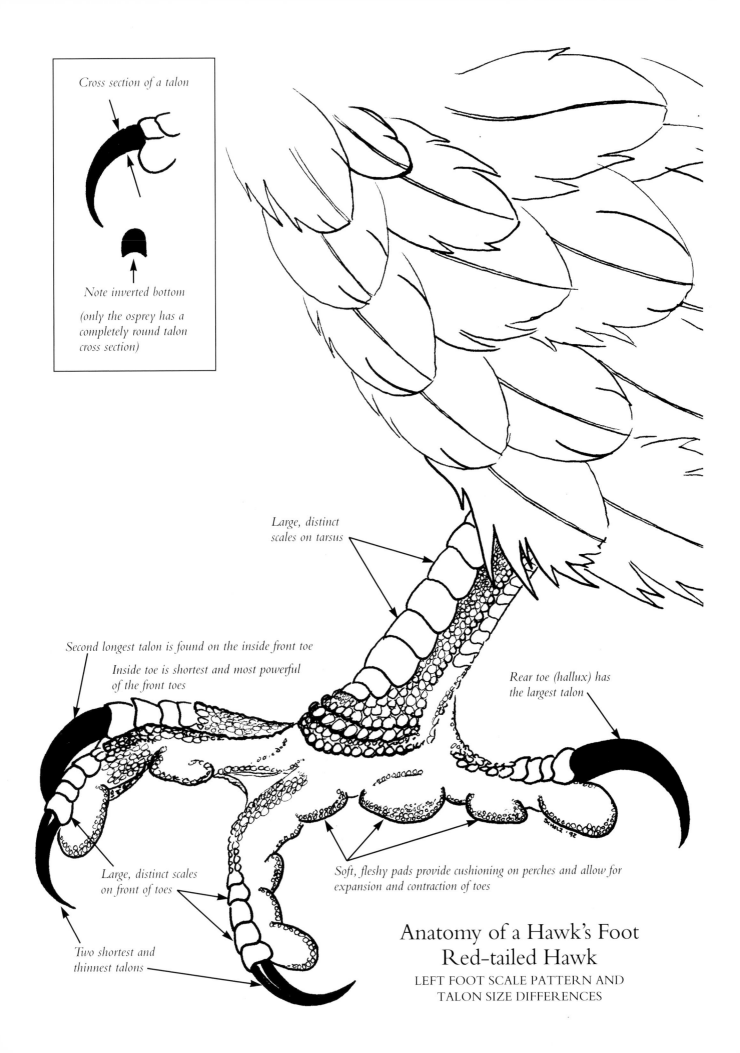

Cross section of a talon

Note inverted bottom

(only the osprey has a completely round talon cross section)

Large, distinct scales on tarsus

Second longest talon is found on the inside front toe

Inside toe is shortest and most powerful of the front toes

Rear toe (hallux) has the largest talon

Large, distinct scales on front of toes

Soft, fleshy pads provide cushioning on perches and allow for expansion and contraction of toes

Two shortest and thinnest talons

Anatomy of a Hawk's Foot
Red-tailed Hawk
LEFT FOOT SCALE PATTERN AND TALON SIZE DIFFERENCES

This male Harris' hawk is perfectly balanced as it rests with one leg tucked neatly into its belly feathers.

When observing live birds, pay close attention to the feet. Note scale shape, size, and configuration and the subtle color variations of different raptor species. As with the bill, a lot of information about a raptor's diet can be learned from the shape, size, and toe configuration of the feet.

You quickly gain respect for the incredible power that these birds possess when you hold them on your fist. Even if you're wearing a heavy leather glove they can get their point across as they shift their weight and adjust their balance, leaving you feeling nothing but pity for the hapless rodent, reptile, or bird that has been targeted for dinner.

Body and Wing Design

A bird of prey must catch and overcome its prey if it is to survive. With this in mind it's not surprising that wing and tail shape and size would vary considerably with the raptor's method of hunting.

The shorter, rounded wings and long tail of the accipiters give them fantastic maneuverability and short, sudden bursts of speed necessary for pursuing prey through heavily wooded habitat. The falcons possess longer tapered and pointed wings and a more compact body, enabling them to achieve some of the fastest speeds of any living organism. What they might lack in maneuverabil-

ity they more than make up for in sheer speed due to a wing shape perfectly suited to the vast openness of the skies in which they hunt. The soaring hawks, or buteos, have broad, rounded wings and broad tails, adaptations that allow them to take full advantage of the rising currents of warm air known as thermals. The buteos can often be seen circling high in the sky in search of prey. As with most larger raptors, their outer five primary feathers are noticeably slotted or notched, creating greater stability in flight. Each feather shaft is rooted in a muscle that independently controls it and makes subtle adjustments as the bird flies.

When you know a raptor's wing shape and flight characteristics, field identification can be made from a distance, even before seeing any of the more obvious field marks such as plumage color. (For more information on raptor wing design, see pages 18–19, 52–53, and 134–135.)

A subadult bald eagle in a relaxed, balanced, upright pose. Note the neck flexibility that allows as much as a 200-degree rotation of the head.

The flaring wings of a subadult bald eagle exhibit distinctly notched outer primaries.

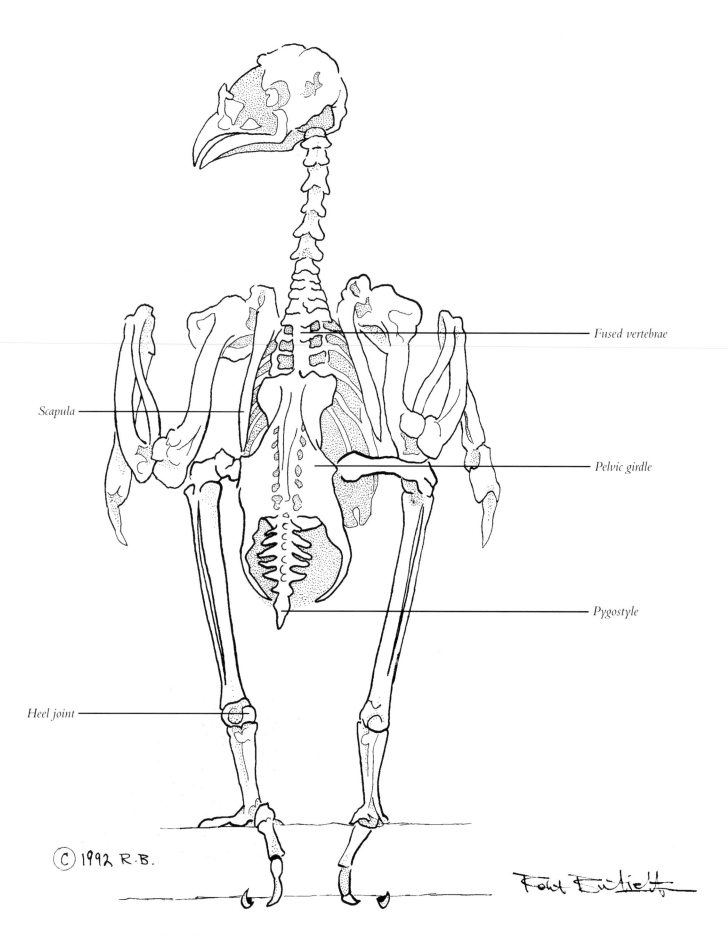

Fused vertebrae

Scapula

Pelvic girdle

Pygostyle

Heel joint

© 1992 R.B.

Skeletal Structure of a Typical Raptor (rear view)

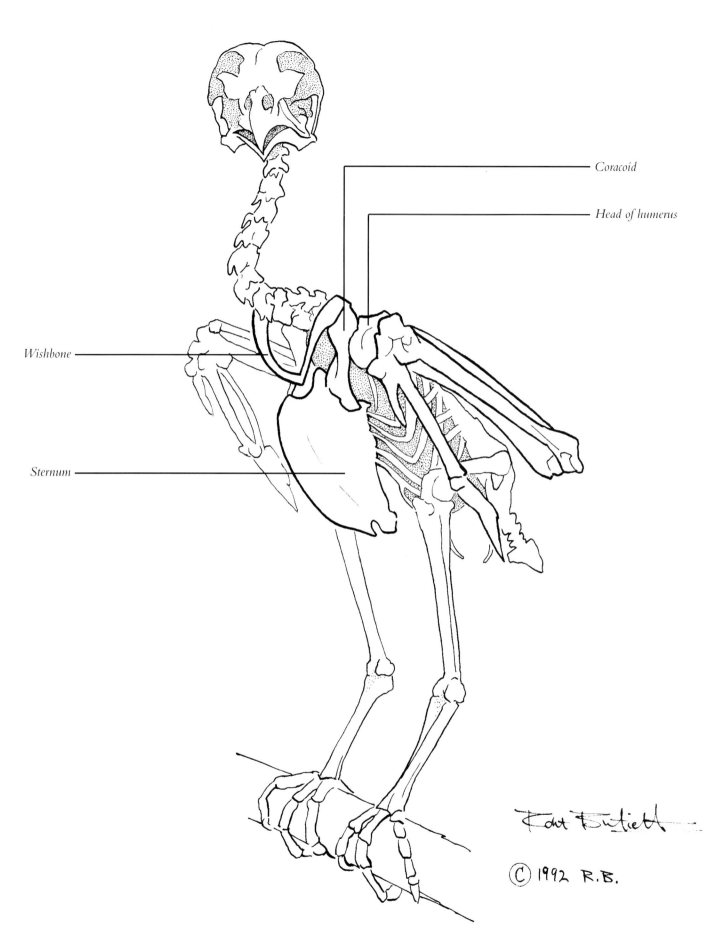

Coracoid

Head of humerus

Wishbone

Sternum

© 1992 R.B.

Skeletal Structure of a Typical Raptor (side view)

High speed and maneuverability are trademarks of a prairie falcon's hunting life. Both are made possible by its long tail and long, pointed, powerful wings.

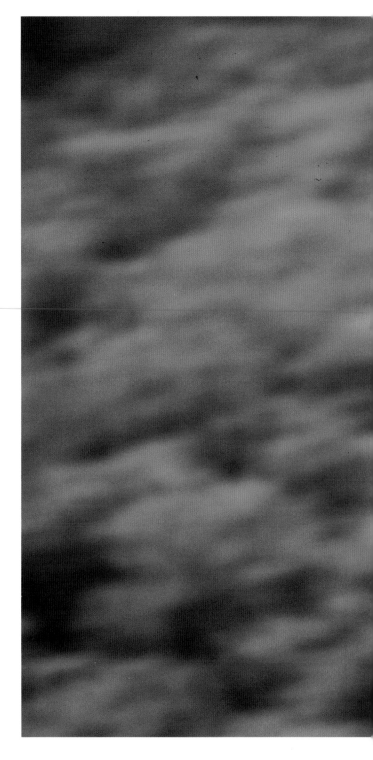

When alarmed, most predatory birds, like this red-tailed hawk, have the ability to raise their hackles or crest feathers to add to their already menacing appearance.

CINDY KILGORE-BROWN

The peregrine zips by low and fast as it zeros in on its next meal.

Following page: Soaring higher and higher into the heavens, this peregrine will gain a height advantage over its prey and use its blinding speed to catch other birds.

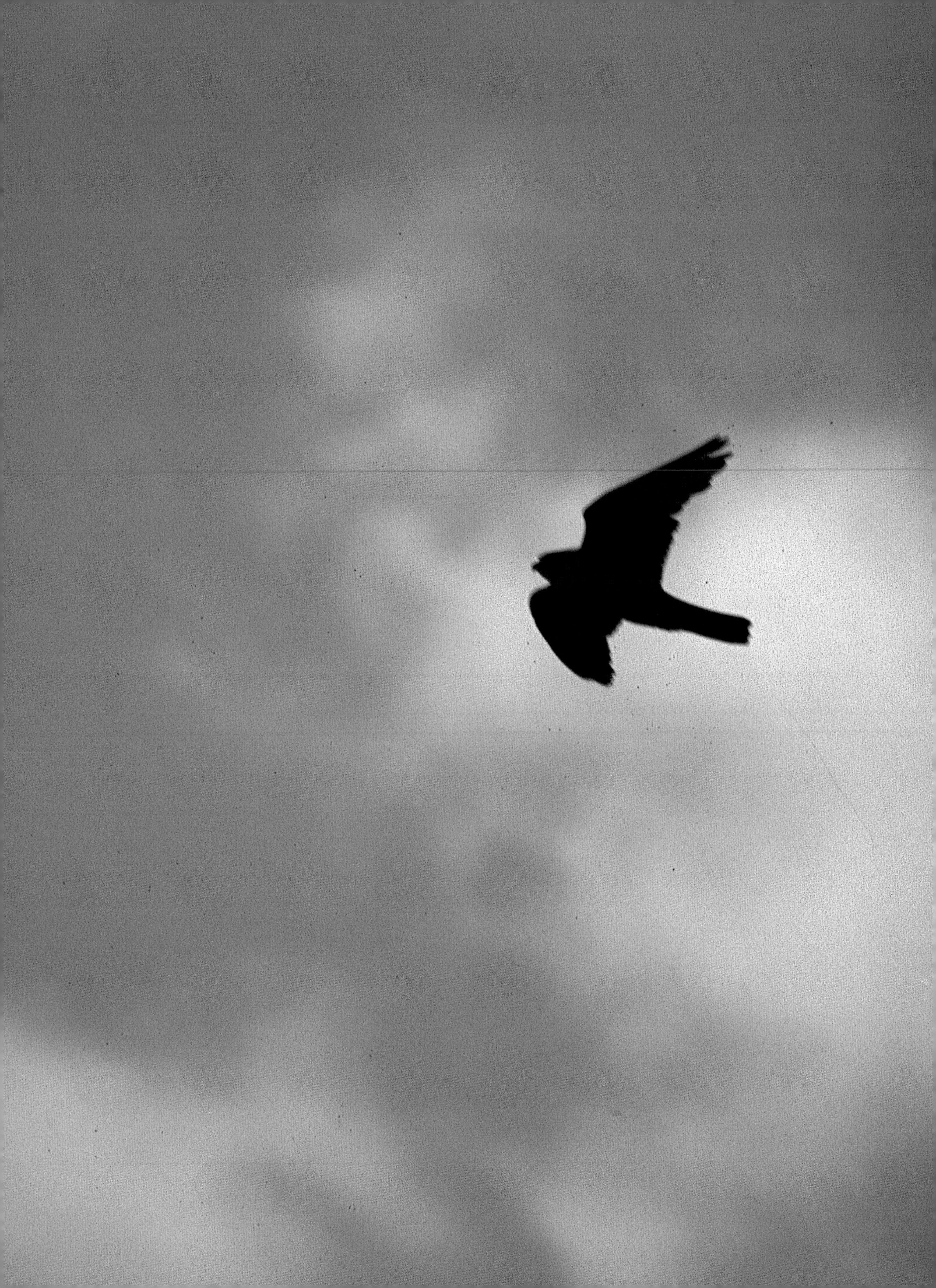

The Species

HAWKS
ACCIPITERS

COOPER'S
Accipiter coóperii

SHARP-SHINNED
Accipiter striátus

NORTHERN GOSHAWK
Accipiter gentilis

REED A. PRESCOTT III

ACCIPITERS

THE THREE NORTH AMERICAN REPRESENTATIVES FROM the worldwide family of accipiters are the sharp-shinned hawk, the Cooper's hawk, and the northern goshawk. Accipiters are quite well-known for their incredible ferocity and high-strung temperament.

With short, rapid wing beats they can speed through even the thickest tangle of forest in pursuit of their feathered quarry. Long, mobile tail feathers and short, rounded wings give the accipiters unparalleled maneuverability.

One of the physical traits contributing to an accipiter's untamable appearance is the intense ruby red color of the adult's eyes. Lacking the heavy furrowed brow of some of the larger hawks, accipiters' eyes seem to bulge out of their heads, giving them an almost maniacal expression.

These hawks are quite solitary and are rarely seen in the wild. Often the only glimpse one gets of an accipiter in the woods is a sudden flash of silver-white underwing lining and the flick of a disappearing tail.

In rural America it is often the Cooper's hawk and the goshawk, and not the hapless red-tail, that are to blame for the commotion in the barnyard. The scenario most likely evolves like this: the farmyard chickens are out in the front yard scratching about for grit when an unsuspecting fowl is snatched up by a goshawk, which disappears into the woods. Hearing the other chickens squawking, the farmer runs out, shotgun in hand, and spots a red-tailed hawk circling overhead in search of rats and mice . . . you can guess the rest.

I'm amazed when I read of the contempt once felt toward the accipiters. Neltje Blanchan, writing of the goshawk in *Birds That Hunt and Are Hunted*, published in 1898, says: "Another villain of deepest dye; what good can be said of it beyond that it wears handsome feathers . . . whitewashing is useless in the case of a bird known to be the most destructive creature on wings." She writes of the sharp-shinned hawk with equal malice: "The so-called 'hen hawks' and 'chicken hawks,' much slandered birds, do not begin to be so destructive as the little reprobate that, like its larger prototype and the equally villainous goshawk, too often escape the charge of shot they so richly deserve." Miss Blanchan goes on to say: "Unhappily, the sharp-shinned hawk is one of the most abundant species we have. Doubtless because it is small and looks inoffensive enough as it soars in narrow circles overhead, its worse than useless life is often spared." It is hard to imagine these are the words of one who at the time considered herself an ornithologist and lover of birds! Thankfully for the accipiters, attitudes have changed so that they are now federally protected and deemed worthy of our admiration and respect.

Trim, sleek, and incredibly well suited for life in the forest, the accipiters are admired for their beauty and refinement and prove a challenging subject for the artist or sculptor.

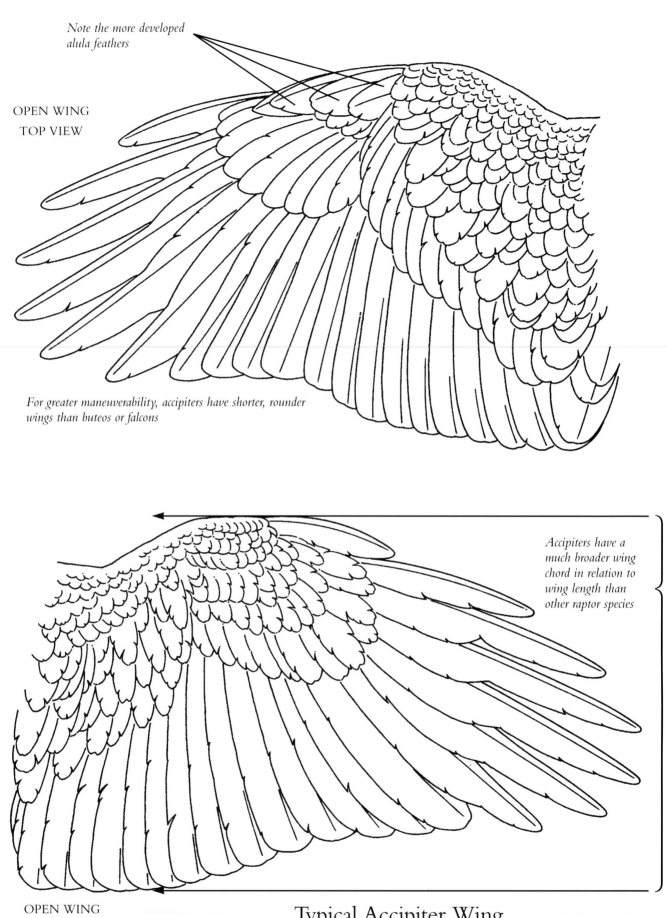

Note the more developed
alula feathers

OPEN WING
TOP VIEW

For greater maneuverability, accipiters have shorter, rounder
wings than buteos or falcons

Accipiters have a
much broader wing
chord in relation to
wing length than
other raptor species

OPEN WING
BOTTOM VIEW

Typical Accipiter Wing
Northern Goshawk
Accipiter gentilis

Sharp-shinned Hawk
Accipiter striatus

SLIGHTLY LARGER THAN A BLUE JAY, THIS FEATHERED dynamo is the smallest nesting accipiter in North America. Feeding primarily on small songbirds, the "sharpie" as it is sometimes called seems perfectly suited to catching food on the wing. At first glance it appears to be nothing more than a scaled-down version of a Cooper's hawk, but on closer examination certain distinctions are obvious. When a sharp-shin is perched on a branch one can see that its tail has a squarish tip, as opposed to the more rounded tail of a Cooper's hawk. Typically a sharpie's plumage is a bit darker on the back of the neck, and the eyes seem quite large in proportion to the head.

Males and females share the same coloration and plumage pattern, but the males may exhibit slightly brighter breast color. One outstanding difference in sexes is the size—the females average about 25 percent larger than the males. This fairly common occurrence among diurnal predatory birds is known as sexual dimorphism. Ornithologists are not sure why it occurs; one of the more popular theories has to do with incubation and nest defense.

The sharp-shinned hawk gets its name from its long, thin legs: the tarsi, or shins, appear to have a leading edge. These long legs aid the hawk in snatching its rather fast, elusive quarry. Although sharp-shins appear delicate they are actually remarkably strong, which decreases a victim's chances of escape once it has been grabbed.

SPECIES PROFILE

1. When sculpting or painting a sharp-shinned hawk, think thin! Sharp-shins are slender, agile raptors. Avoid the tendency to portray them as robust.
2. Adults achieve the red eye color after their second to third year of maturity. Immature eye color can vary from olive green to pale yellow.
3. When folded, the wings extend to about the midsection of the tail.
4. Juvenile and second-year birds are dark brownish on the back and have subtle brown streaking through the chest and breast areas.
5. Sharp-shins have unusually long, thin legs and toes in relation to body size.
6. The tail is squarish at the tip when folded but appears quite round when spread.
7. The cere and feet are pale yellow on adults. On juveniles these areas are flesh-toned or slightly olive.
8. Females average about 13 to 14 inches long, while males average 11 to 12 inches.
9. Hunting techniques vary, but sharp-shins are often seen rocketing through thick hedgerows bordering fields and open forest.
10. Small birds and occasional rodents make up a large part of the sharp-shin's diet.

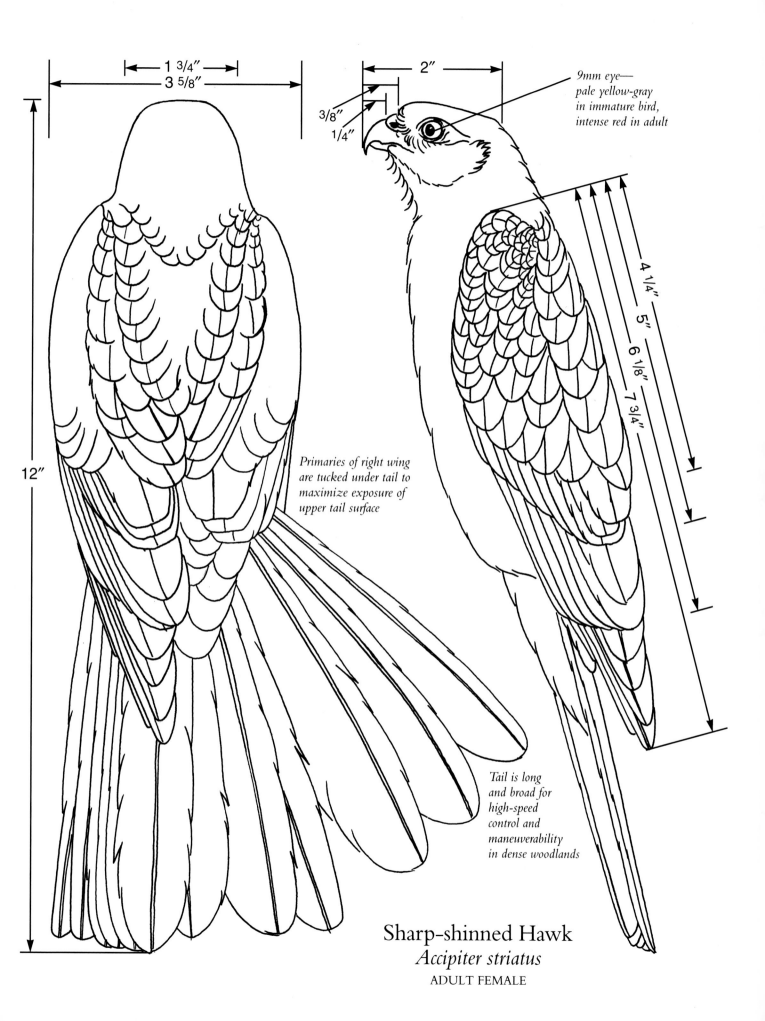

1 3/4"

3 5/8"

2"

3/8"

1/4"

9mm eye—
pale yellow-gray
in immature bird,
intense red in adult

12"

4 1/4"

5"

6 1/8"

7 3/4"

Primaries of right wing
are tucked under tail to
maximize exposure of
upper tail surface

Tail is long
and broad for
high-speed
control and
maneuverability
in dense woodlands

Sharp-shinned Hawk

Accipiter striatus

ADULT FEMALE

Its sleek body, long tail, and large eyes all contribute to the sharp-shinned hawk's ability to hunt in even the thickest forest growth.

Long, thin legs give the sharp-shinned hawk its name.

These two study skins show the dramatic size difference between the larger female and a male in immature plumage.

Plumage patterns vary considerably between immature and adult accipiters, especially on the belly and breast feathers, as with these two males.

The large round eye, compact head, and lighter gray top of the head are some of the chief distinguishing features of the sharp-shin.

Heavily barred wings and tail and beautifully patterned breast and belly areas are evident on the undersides of this adult male sharp-shin.

The extremely long alula feathers on the underside of the wing aid in maneuverability and stabilization during flight.

The notching on the outer edges of the first five primary feathers is known as emargination. Note how beautifully all the feather groups overlap one another.

Large, bulbous eyes and a sharply hooked bill mark the sharp-shin as an accipiter. Note the large nostril openings and the distinct feather flow around the eyes.

Sexual dimorphism in size occurs in most of the bird-eating hawks and falcons.

The feathers on top of the head more closely resemble fur. Note the stiff rictal bristles that originate from the lore area in front of the eyes and flow up and onto the cere.

This full back view shows the various feather groups and how they relate to one another. Note the white patch on the back of the neck. This white area is quite visible when the sharp-shinned hawk becomes agitated and raises its crest feathers.

Cooper's Hawk
Accipiter cooperii

IN CONTRAST TO ITS SMALLER COUSIN, THE SHARP-shinned hawk, the Cooper's hawk seems to prefer hunting in a less congested environment. The Cooper's is an incredibly beautiful creature, extremely well proportioned, a seemingly perfect combination of size, color, and form. It hunts deciduous forests and mixed cleared areas throughout North America and Canada. Short is the life span of any small to medium-sized bird that flies across the path of a hungry Cooper's hawk! This raptor will sit patiently for hours in a tree waiting to spy its prey. With blinding speed and accuracy the Cooper's hawk maneuvers in for the attack, attempting to remain as inconspicuous as possible until the last minute. Rabbits, mice, and other small animals also figure into the Cooper's hawk's diet and are often snatched as the hungry accipiter cruises along forest edges and clearings.

Possessing all the classic accipiter traits—short, rounded wings, a comparatively small head, and a long, darkly barred tail (which, unlike the sharp-shin's, is more rounded at the tip when folded)—this dashing bird of prey is truly a living, breathing work of art.

Officially named Cooper's hawk in 1828 after prominent New York naturalist William Cooper, this 15- to 20-inch hawk can occasionally be an unwelcome guest at the backyard bird feeder, where a high concentration of easy pickings proves an irresistible target.

SPECIES PROFILE

1. The Cooper's hawk looks like the sharp-shin but is slightly more robust in appearance and slightly larger. A male Cooper's hawk and a female sharp-shin can be quite similar in size.
2. The eyes are proportionately smaller in relation to head size than those of a sharpie.
3. The tail is long and rounded at the tip.
4. Note the whitish area directly behind the top of the head.
5. Adults are steel blue through the back area. The eyes are red, and the cere, legs, and toes are pale yellow.
6. Immature Cooper's hawks are streaked with brown throughout the belly and breast area and are uniform medium brown above; the eyes are pale yellow.
7. With wings folded the primaries extend not quite halfway down the length of the tail.
8. The Cooper's hawk prefers to hunt in fairly open areas, watching for prey from a concealed perch.

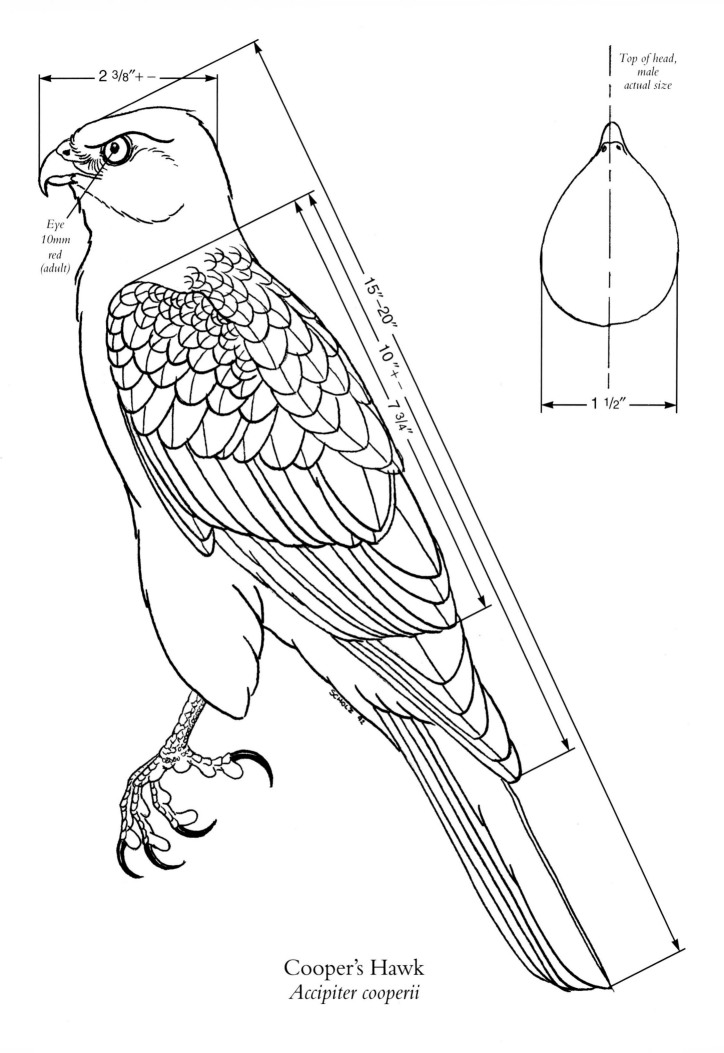

2 3/8"+ −

Eye
10mm
red
(adult)

Top of head,
male
actual size

15"-20"

10 "+ −

7 3/4"

1 1/2"

SCHOLZ 91

Cooper's Hawk
Accipiter cooperii

The intense, blood red eye and trim, elegant form are hallmarks of the adult Cooper's hawk.

Note the relationship between the shoulder feathers and the chest feathers and how they overlap at points of convergence. Also pictured is the feather flow around the eyes and bill.

The tarsus feathers, or "pants," originate quite high up toward the breast area. Note the long alula visible on the left wing.

The feathering on the top of the head of an adult Cooper's hawk is much darker than that of its smaller cousin the sharp-shin.

The shoulder and scapular feathers flow up and overlap the wing down to the tertial feathers.

A Cooper's hawk striking a defiant pose. Note the beautiful patterns of the chest feathers and how they flow gracefully onto the belly area.

The extremely well-developed alula feathers are visible in this mantling pose. Note the broad wing cord, the distance from the wrist to the ends of the secondary feathers.

As the wing folds, the primary coverts and alula feathers slide neatly under the secondary coverts and upper wing feathers of the wrist.

A left-side profile of an adult Cooper's hawk. Note the scapular feathers cascading onto the upper wing surface.

Arcing from the lower chin up to the eyes, the facial feathers seem to frame the face. These feathers are structured quite differently from the broader platelike feathers of the neck and shoulder areas.

The long, thin tarsi and feet as well as the fluffy undertail coverts are evident in this picture of an alert Cooper's hawk.

The broad webbing between the outer and middle toes is obvious in this photo, as are the light scale patterns on the toes.

The upper wing covert feathers are laid out in neat, uniform rows as shown on the partially opened left wing.

The leading edge of the wrist area shows a distinct color change from steel blue above to silvery white below. Note the soft convergence of the two feather groups on the side of the neck.

Broad, rounded wings propel the Cooper's hawk along at remarkably fast speeds in pursuit of prey. Note the short, round shape of the smaller upper wing coverts and how they contrast with the long, well-developed primary and secondary feather groups.

The silvery barring gets progressively lighter toward the body.

Northern Goshawk
Accipiter gentilis

IN ATTEMPTING TO DESCRIBE THE REPUTATION AND legendary hunting prowess of this amazing bird, I am hard pressed to come up with a single adjective. Bloodthirsty, savage, ruthless, elegant, and marvelous can all be used to describe this feathered thunderbolt of a bird.

Measuring from 21 to 26 inches in length, the goshawk is the largest and most powerful of the accipiters. This raptor is famous for its tenacity in the pursuit of prey, making it a favorite of many falconers. If looks could kill, the goshawk would have to expend very little energy to obtain a meal.

An adult goshawk is truly a sight to behold. It is largely gray-blue with a blood red eye and a striking white stripe over a lightly furrowed brow. The chest, breast, and belly areas are silvery white and heavily vermiculated with light brownish gray patterns. The sturdy legs and solid toes are pale yellow and tipped with black daggerlike talons. Not a terribly fussy diner, the goshawk will prey on just about anything that it feels it can subdue, with grouse and rabbits making up a large part of its diet.

Because goshawks are one of the few wild creatures that demonstrate little fear of humans, especially during the nesting season, they have a well-earned reputation for ferocity. Documented reports abound of careless hikers wandering near an active goshawk nest who have been persistently divebombed and occasionally struck by an angry female anxious to resume her parental duties in solitude.

SPECIES PROFILE

1. The goshawk's plumage is a subtle gray-blue with distinct whitish undersides and a heavily vermiculated breast and belly area.
2. The tail is long and slightly rounded.
3. The open wings are distinctly rounded. When folded they extend just less than half the tail length.
4. The legs and toes appear stouter and thicker in relation to body size than those of the sharp-shinned and Cooper's hawks.
5. Adults have a distinct white eye stripe over the brow ridge, red eyes, pale yellow cere and feet, and dark slate crown and back.
6. Immature goshawks are pale brown above and heavily streaked with brown below. Their eyes are pale yellow.
7. Goshawks feed on a variety of small to medium-sized birds, mammals, and even reptiles.
8. Extremely fast and maneuverable fliers, goshawks can zip through even the thickest forest with only a slight disturbance to the surrounding tree branches. They hunt the thick green northern forests of the United States and Canada, but when prey is scarce they will move to hunt southern territories.

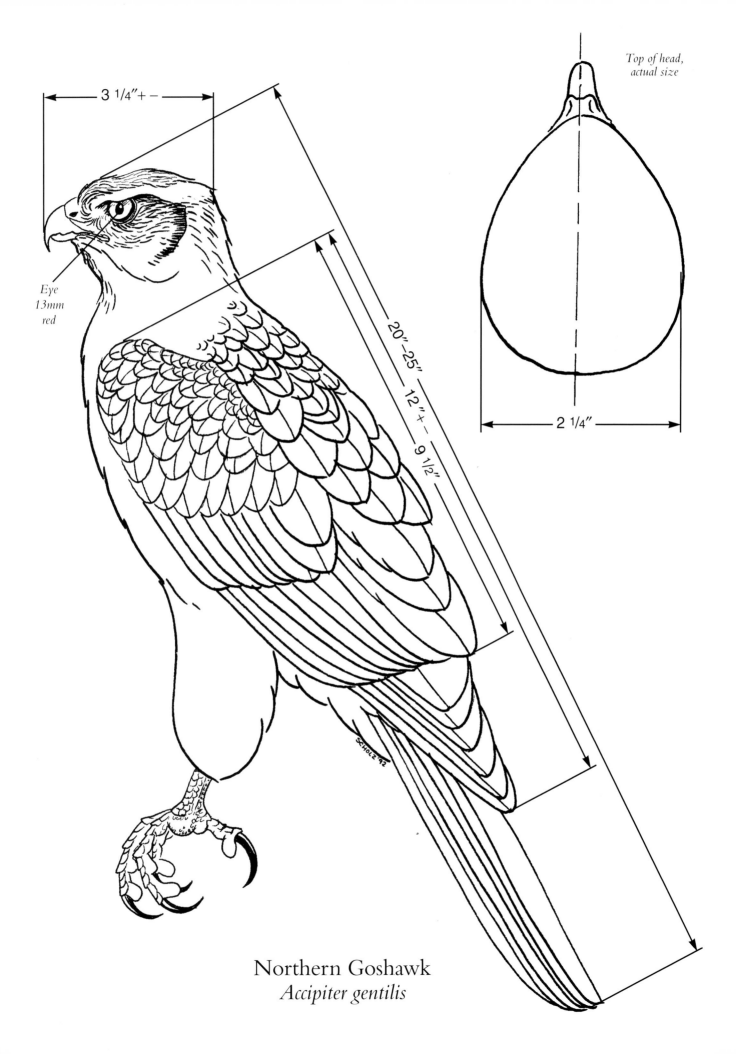

3 1/4"+ −

Eye
13mm
red

20"-25"

12"+ −

9 1/2"

Top of head,
actual size

2 1/4"

SCHOLZ '92

Northern Goshawk
Accipiter gentilis

This close-up of a goshawk's head and neck shows the open mouth and sharply hooked upper mandible.

A front view showing the powerful hunched shoulders and the soft, flowing, furlike feathers of the undertail coverts.

The partially exposed alula feathers are rooted in the wrist of the wing. Note the dark feather shafts of the upper wing coverts.

Note the fleshy lobe protruding from the eyebrow. Eye color varies from blood red to the light orange-brown pictured here.

Sleek cheek and throat feathers flow into the heavily vermiculated chest feathers.

The fleshy lobes of the toes are visible in this photo.

Cryptic patterning and the partially exposed alula feather can be seen on the underside of the right wing's leading edge.

As the goshawk spreads its wings to regain balance, the distinct color change between the upper and lower wing surfaces becomes quite clear. Note the size difference on the front toes between the inner and middle talons.

The wide spacing of the legs and extremely powerful feet allow the goshawk to catch and overcome large and heavy prey such as rabbits and grouse.

Note the narrow bill and cere and the "pinched" look at the corners of the mouth.

This three-quarter view shows the shape, color, and relationships of the scapulars, tertials, and secondary feathers.
Also notice the hunching of the upper shoulders as the bird
looks down.

Opposite page: An adult goshawk in
immaculate plumage. The short primary
feathers extend only halfway down the
tail.

The long neck allows for 200-degree rotation of the head.
Note the beautiful feather patterns of the major flight feathers
and back area.

Heavy leather jesses are a necessity when training and working with such a powerful raptor as the goshawk.

The white eye stripes gradually trail off and broaden toward the back of the head. Note the extremely dark coloring on the top of the head.

Opposite page: The long, darkly barred tail is tipped with white, as are the upper tail coverts, or rump feathers.

The distance from the wrist to the top of the primaries is relatively short on this specimen. It also has a heavily vermiculated chest and belly area, and the silvery underside of the tail is unbarred.

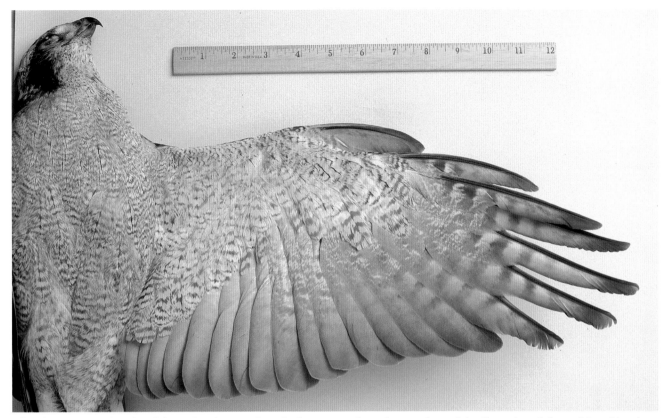

The silvery gray undersides of the goshawk's secondary feathers are not barred as are those of the Cooper's and sharp-shinned hawks.

The upper surfaces of all the major flight feathers are brown instead of the gray-blue of the rest of the wing and back areas.

FALCONS

PEREGRINE
*Fálco
peregrínus*

AMERICAN
KESTREL
*Fálco
sparvérius*

KESTREL – IMMATURE
A RETRACTED HEAD CHANGES
SHAPE + ATTITUDE OF BIRD

GYRFALCON
Fálco rustícolus

MERLIN
Fálco columbáris

PRAIRIE
Fálco mexicánus

Falcons

=====================

WORLDWIDE THE TRUE FALCONS COMPRISE SOME sixty species, ranging in size from the tiny African pygmy falcon not much larger than a house sparrow up to the majestic gyrfalcon, which can attain lengths of up to 24 inches. In North America, the family Falconidae is represented by seven species, including the crested caracara and aplomado falcon. This chapter will deal only with the five most familiar: the kestrel, merlin, prairie falcon, peregrine falcon, and gyrfalcon.

Several physical distinctions shared by most falcons set them apart from other hawklike birds. Immediately apparent is the lack of a heavy brow, or superciliary ridge. This combined with large, soft, round eyes gives these birds a less threatening appearance. Falcon eye color, unlike that of most other diurnal raptors of North America, does not change from juvenile to adult. Long, pointed wings and distinctive flight patterns make falcons easier to identify in the field than some other raptors.

Another physical attribute of falcons is a bony baffle, or tubercle, located in the nostril opening. This is believed to be an adaptation to facilitate breathing at high speeds. Renowned for their aerial prowess, certain falcons are known to be the fastest creatures on the planet. While in a vertical dive or stoop, peregrine falcons are capable of attaining speeds up to 160 miles an hour.

Bill structure and design also set falcons apart from other raptors. They all have a notch or tomial tooth on the upper mandible. It is thought that this tooth allows for a more efficient dispatch of their prey, which tend to be of the avian variety, by severing the neck vertebrae. Falcons, unlike hawks and eagles, tend to use the bill as well as their powerful talons to overcome and kill prey.

Hunting technique differs greatly from species to species. American kestrels have a habit of hovering over open meadows in search of insects and mice. Merlins rely on their great speed in overcoming prey in direct pursuit. Prairie falcons and especially peregrines are famous for their spectacular aerial stoops from great altitudes, rocketing downward on tightly folded wings. The gyrfalcon usually relies on the element of surprise, flying low and using the terrain to conceal its approach until it is upon its unsuspecting victim. But gyrfalcons are quite capable of catching even the swiftest quarry in a straight-line, level pursuit if the occasion arises.

Falcons are creatures of elegance and beauty. It is not surprising that they have played such an importantly symbolic role in the development of human civilization. In the medieval days the particular species of falcon one was permitted to own was directly correlated with one's position in society; thus, the higher one's social standing, the larger the falcon, with the pure white arctic gyrfalcons reserved only for kings and emperors.

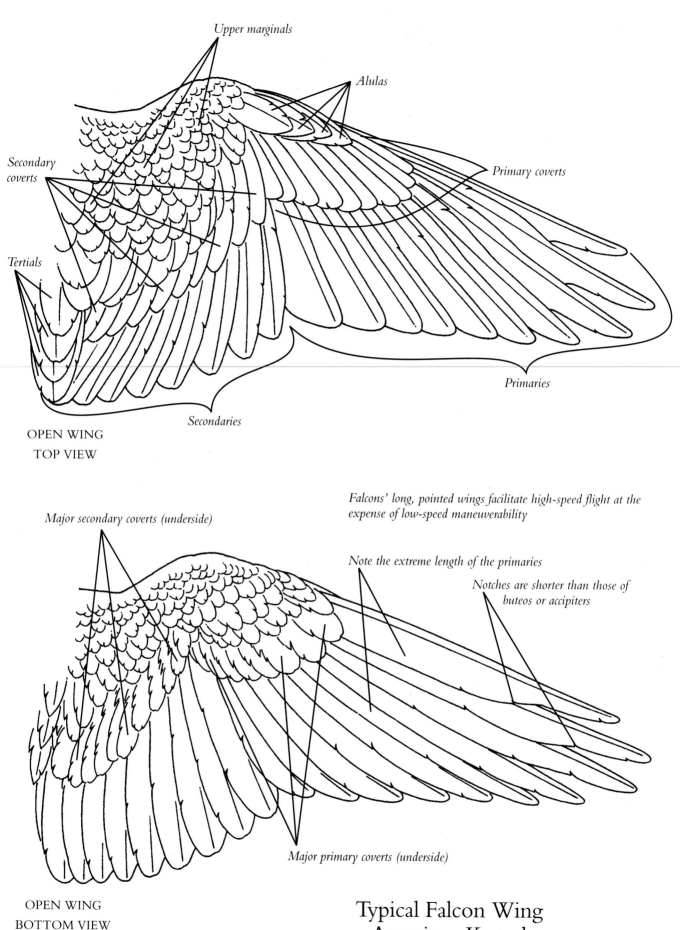

Upper marginals

Alulas

Secondary coverts

Primary coverts

Tertials

Primaries

Secondaries

OPEN WING
TOP VIEW

Major secondary coverts (underside)

Falcons' long, pointed wings facilitate high-speed flight at the expense of low-speed maneuverability

Note the extreme length of the primaries

Notches are shorter than those of buteos or accipiters

Major primary coverts (underside)

OPEN WING
BOTTOM VIEW

Typical Falcon Wing
American Kestrel
Falco sparverius

American Kestrel
Falco sparverius

THE AMERICAN KESTREL IS QUITE POSSIBLY THE MOST abundant bird of prey in North America. This small, brightly colored falcon is able to adapt and even proliferate alongside human development; this ability has no doubt contributed to its survival success as a species. The kestrel's acceptance of artificial nest boxes and its varied dietary requirements make it one of the more easily observable North American raptors. Here in Vermont kestrels are commonly seen perched on telephone lines bordering empty fields, constantly on the lookout for insects, small snakes, and mice, all of which make up a large part of their diet. At first glance it's quite easy to mistake a perched kestrel for an equally sized mourning dove, but the kestrel's habits of bobbing its head and twitching its tail aid in quick identification.

With most hawks, eagles, and falcons the male, or tiercel, is the smaller of the sexes. Unlike most other raptors, the male kestrel's plumage is distinctly different from that of the female. Head and facial markings are similar, but the tiercel has deep blue-gray upper wing coverts (the shoulder area) heavily marked by black, squarish, teardrop-shaped spots. The tail of the adult tiercel lacks the heavy barring of the female; it usually has just one wide subterminal band and a white tip. The female appears much larger and browner overall.

The kestrel hunts by perching up high and patiently waiting for prey to appear. It will also hover over a clearing, and once a potential meal has been spotted, the kestrel pounces, dispatching the victim with a quick bite to the head or neck.

During breeding and courtship it is not uncommon to hear the kestrel's piercing "killey, killey, killey" call before seeing it.

Considering the bird's relatively small size, beautiful colors, and endearing personality, it is not surprising that the American kestrel is such a popular subject of bird artists—kestrels usually far outnumber other raptors in the bird-of-prey categories at carving shows.

SPECIES PROFILE

1. Kestrels have large, round brown eyes with distinct dark malar (cheek) stripes.
2. Males (or tiercels) have a very distinct, rust-colored round patch on the top of the head.
3. The back and tail are rufous brown with black barring on females; males have one large black bar at the end of the tail.
4. The wings are long and pointed with black and white spots underneath.
5. The head is large and round; the kestrel has a habit of bobbing its head and twitching its tail when perched.
6. The bill is deep bluish black at the tip and heavily notched.
7. Dark "eye spots" are visible on the back of the head.
8. Tiercels have blue-gray shoulders and distinct black spots along the sides of the breast and flanks.
9. Both sexes are bright yellow on the cere, eye lobes, and feet.
10. Males measure from 9 to 10 inches, females from 11 to 12 inches.

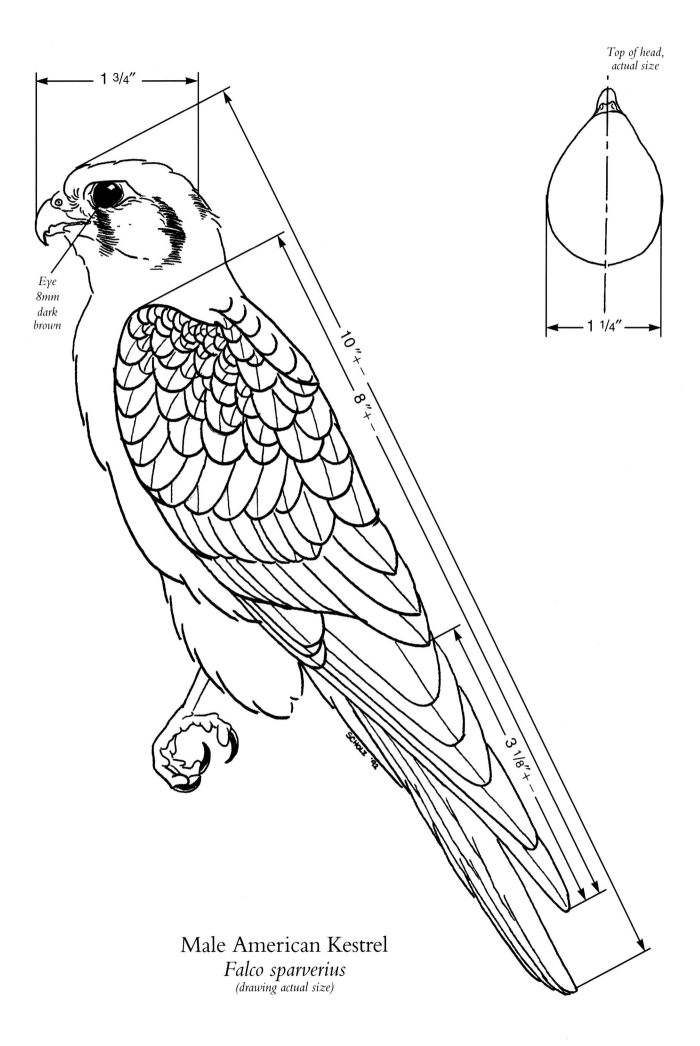

1 3/4″

Eye
8mm
dark
brown

10″+

8″+

3 1/8″+

SCHOLZ '88

Top of head,
actual size

1 1/4″

Male American Kestrel
Falco sparverius
(drawing actual size)

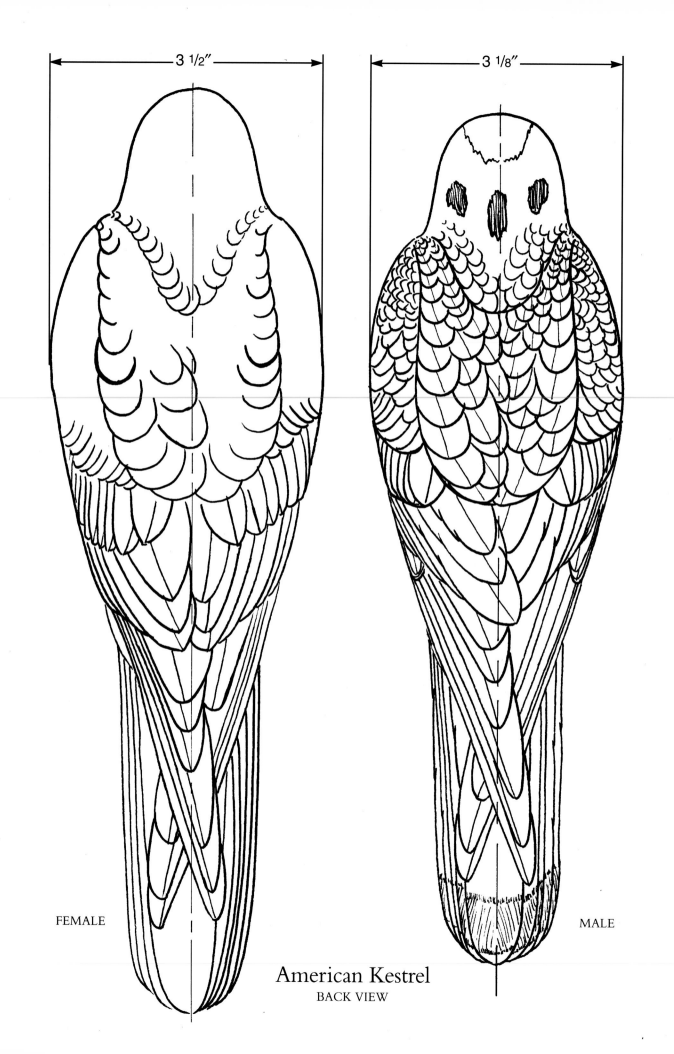

3 1/2"

3 1/8"

FEMALE

MALE

American Kestrel
BACK VIEW

This close-up of a relaxed, "puffed up" male kestrel shows the delicate feathering and extraordinary coloring of the face and head area. Note the furlike texture of the feathers.

The eye-to-bill relationship is evident in this front view. This particular kestrel has a slightly enlarged left nostril.

A close-up of the eye area illustrates both the feather flow around the eye and the feather structure, which is especially evident in the white cheek feathers that overlap the dark stripe behind the eye.

The back of a male kestrel's head exhibits distinct "eye spots."

A well-proportioned head profile. Note the distinct shape of the eyelid and the bright yellow coloring of the fleshy lobe in front of the eye.

Bright white edges can be seen on the tips of all the major flight feathers.

This front view of an alert male kestrel shows the unique black "polka dots" on the belly and flank feathers.

Occasionally the upper chest feathers overlap onto the wrist area of the wing.

The long primary feathers can cross as far up as the base of the tail. Note the distinction between the tertial feather group and the secondary feathers.

Detail of the right foot and toes. Note the scale pattern on the top of the toes and how the scales decrease in size toward the leg.

Opposite page: When viewed from the back, the kestrel's falcon characteristics are obvious: long, narrow wings, a streamlined shape, and long tail. Note how the scapular feathers overlap onto the wings.

Like all birds of prey, the kestrel has an extremely flexible and maneuverable neck allowing the full rotation of the head.

JACK MURRAY

This little male fluffs up against the cold winter winds.

As this curious little kestrel leans forward slightly, the tarsus feathers begin to protrude from the belly feathers. The growth patterns, or "scalloping," of the upper mandible can be seen in this view.

The balance point of this semialert bird is directly behind the head. To locate the balance point draw a vertical line straight up from the balls of the feet.

Three distinct zones of feather growth are apparent here: the chin, the breast, and the belly feathers.

Male kestrels have a unique rust-colored patch directly on top of the head.

The three-quarters extension of this male kestrel's wing shows the distinctive coloration and patterns of the upper surface.

Above and opposite page: This sequence of photos shows the underside of a wing slowly opening to reveal the full shape and location of each of the major flight feathers and how they relate to one another.

At first glance you might notice little difference between the male and female kestrel. Both bear the distinctive black malar stripes and facial markings seen in this front view of a male.

A close-up of the side of the head clearly shows eyelid detail and the graceful feather flow around the eye.

Note: The following photographs depict a female kestrel.

This back view shows the placement of the black eye spots and the heavily barred wrist and shoulder area.

This view shows the tight, pinched look at the corners of the bill. Note the subtle transition from the pure white chin feathers to the heavily streaked upper chest.

The male kestrel's head feathers are extremely colorful. There is less contrast between the rust colored patch and the surrounding blue feathers on the top of the female's head.

Aside from the difference in size, one of the distinguishing field marks of a female kestrel is a lack of blue upper wing coverts.

A female kestrel's breast, belly, and flanks are heavily streaked with soft brown markings. Note the almost furlike quality of the feathers.

As this female turns her head to look over her shoulder, note how the entire grouping of head feathers moves as a complete unit independent of her body feathers, yet the pattern flows smoothly between head and body.

Unlike the male, the female kestrel has a heavily barred upper tail.

The kestrel turns to look up, accentuating the feathers on the back of her head. Note the eye and the bulbous shape of the lens.

The stretched right wing exposes the primary feathers and primary coverts. Note the pronounced alula feathers. This photo is an excellent study of wing shape and the relationship of feather groups.

With the leather jesse lifted up and out of the way, you can see the distinctive colors and patterns on the kestrel's leg and foot. Despite its relatively small size, the kestrel possesses a remarkably strong grip.

The nostril is positioned directly in front of the eye. This important detail is true for most falcons.

Clearly visible in this picture are the balance point and wing feather layout. The bird is molting new top tail feathers, which accounts for their shorter length.

Opposite page: This head close-up of a female American kestrel highlights the furlike quality of the head feathers and shows eye and bill details.

A full-body front view of an adult female American kestrel. Female kestrels differ from males or tiercels not only in size but also in plumage patterns and colors.

Opposite page: In this full front view, a female American kestrel stands with her outer toes in the high arch position. Incorporating subtle details like this adds authenticity to your portrayal of the species.

Merlin
Falco columbarius

LIKE ITS LARGER COUSIN THE GYRFALCON, THE MERLIN seems to prefer life in the North. Occasionally found nesting south of the Canadian border, this blue-jay-sized powerhouse is most often observed along coastal migration routes during its spring and fall journeys where, with blinding speed, it commonly picks off unfortunate shorebirds and songbirds.

On the Massachusetts coast I once saw a merlin fly into a flock of dunlins and emerge from the other side with a dunlin grasped in each foot. Merlins are versatile hunters. They are as adept at high-level stoops as they are at low-level straight-on pursuits. Small birds make up almost all of a merlin's diet. In appearance, merlins resemble scaled-down peregrine falcons with big eyes. Adult males have white breasts and bellies heavily streaked with brown, and slate blue backs with dark central shafts on most of the feathers. The sides of the face are streaked with brown, showing only a subtle malar (or cheek-area) stripe under the eye. Female merlins appear only slightly larger than males and have a more brownish appearance.

Coloration may vary greatly depending on geographic region. Back color may graduate from a light powder blue to almost blue-black in some West Coast morphs.

The merlin is truly an international bird. It is found throughout North America, Greenland, Northern Europe, and Russia nesting in a variety of dense, coniferous woodland habitats.

It seems strange that a bird with such seemingly perfect survival qualities—its body proportions, ferocious nature, and eating habits—isn't more widespread and common throughout its range.

═══ SPECIES PROFILE ═══

1. In overall appearance the merlin resembles a scaled-down, compact peregrine falcon.
2. It ranges in size from 9 to 12 inches.
3. Rapid wing beats distinguish its flight pattern.
4. The facial pattern and breast area are heavily streaked with brown.
5. The eyes are extremely large and dark brown.
6. Note the wide, stocky-shouldered "tough guy" stance.
7. The tail is black and white with heavy barring.
8. The primaries are edged with white.
9. Females, with their overall brown color, appear much more somber in coloration than males.
10. Both sexes have long, thin toes that aid in capturing avian prey.

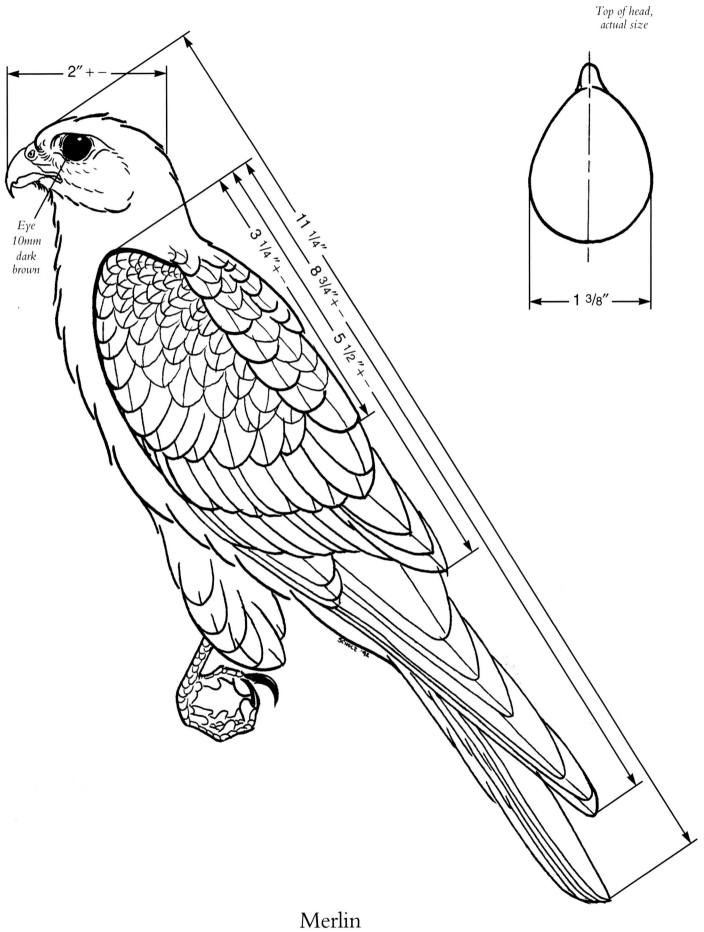

Top of head,
actual size

2" + −

Eye
10mm
dark
brown

11 1/4"

8 3/4" + −

3 1/4" + −

5 1/2" + −

1 3/8"

SCHOLZ '92

Merlin
Falco columbarius

The head of an adult merlin exhibits brown streaking around the eye and onto the cheek area.

The merlin has a large eye and slightly elongated bill. Its head is distinctly more wedge-shaped than that of the American kestrel.

This full front view shows the wrist area and the whole belly and breast. Note the large spidery feet and the way the toes come in contact with the branch.

Heavy brown streaking is prominent throughout the upper breast area.

The soft-edged feathers flow from the breast down onto the belly area between the legs.

The long, sinuous toes have distinct ball-like pads under each joint and are tipped with needle sharp talons.

This bird is molting in new feathers. The primaries will grow until they almost touch the end of the tail.

The dark brown and white streaking continues around the back of the head and onto the nape.

A three-quarter back view showing the right wing and all the back feather groups.

JACK MURRAY

JACK MURRAY

Right: Out on a limb this immature merlin goes through a series of stretching exercises.

JACK MURRAY

A nice view of the interior of the underwing, the axillary feathers, and the long flank feathers that flow over the leg. Note how the wing joins the body up near the neck area.

A three-quarter view of the upper back from below.

The upper left shoulder feathers are covered by the chin and upper breast feathers when the merlin turns its head to look over its shoulder.

During the molt the old feathers drop off and are replaced by new ones. The outside tail feathers of this merlin are growing in pairs on both sides of the tail.

This back view shows juvenile brown feathers gradually being replaced by the gray-blue plumage of an adult.

Opposite page: Notice the inside of the leg and how the upper section of the leg extends up the front, almost touching the breast.

Prairie Falcon
Falco mexicanus

THIS HANDSOME, DUSKY BROWN, MIDSIZED FALCON hunts the arid deserts and exposed cliffs overlooking rivers and canyons of the western United States.

A favorite among western falconers, the prairie falcon is not as highly specialized in its choice of prey as some other members of the falcon family. Jackrabbits, gophers, and even occasional snakes figure in its diet, although in most cases small birds make up a large portion of a prairie falcon's menu. Its hunting technique differs from that of its close cousin the peregrine falcon: prairies are more likely to use low-level surprise assaults on their quarry and rely less on the high-altitude stoops employed by peregrines.

In flight a prairie falcon is recognizable by its typical falcon silhouette (long, pointed wings and relatively small, compact head). Upon closer observation the armpit area (axillary area) is distinctly dark brown up to the wrist, giving the wing underside a dark-and-light patchwork appearance.

Although its breeding range is limited to the western desert areas of the United States, in the areas where it is found the prairie falcon can be quite common. Prairie falcons rarely nest anywhere but on cliff faces and steep canyon walls overlooking vast river basins. Often the area below an active prairie falcon nest is brightly whitewashed with droppings, allowing for easy discovery by a well-trained eye.

═ SPECIES PROFILE ═

1. The prairie falcon, which measures from 15 to 18 inches, is a dusty brown, long-winged desert falcon.
2. The large, round, dark brown eyes are quite evident.
3. A dark brown malar stripe extends down to the throat area.
4. The cere and feet are pale yellow in adults, pale blue in juveniles.
5. No color phases exist, although first-year birds do appear darker.
6. The profile of a prairie falcon is slightly smaller and trimmer than that of its close cousin the peregrine.
7. The head tends to be much more angular in shape than that of other falcons.
8. The prairie falcon hunts in a low-level direct pursuit. It feeds on a variety of small birds, rodents, and even reptiles.
9. It nests on high cliffs overlooking valleys and rivers.

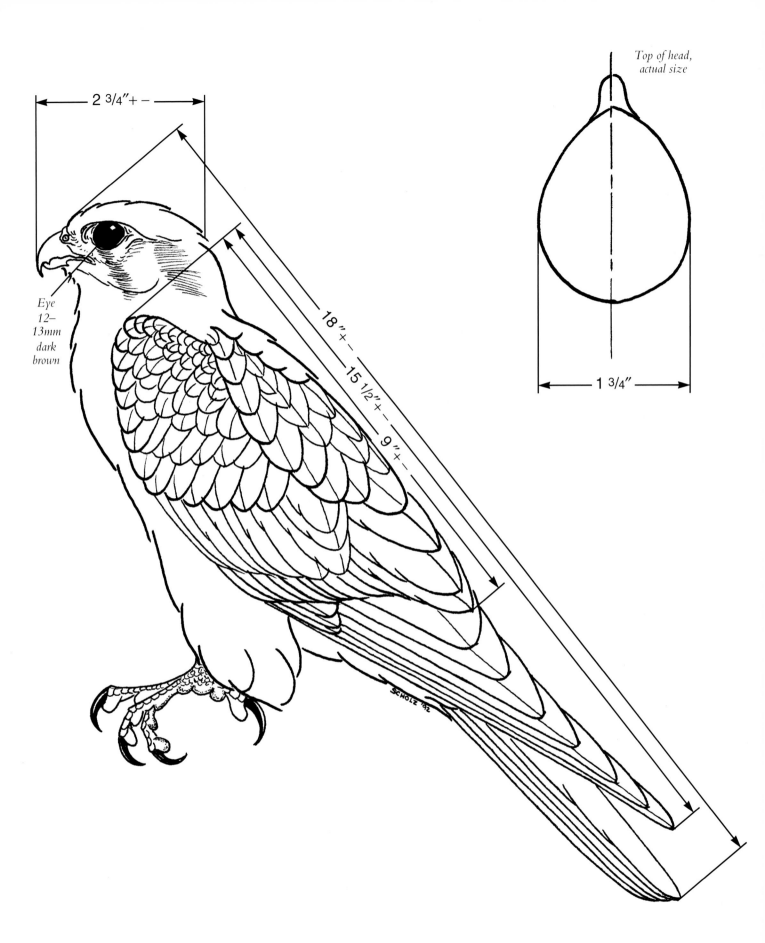

2 3/4"+ –

Eye
12–
13mm
dark
brown

18"+ –
15 1/2"+ –
9"+ –

SCHOLZ '92

Top of head,
actual size

1 3/4"

Prairie Falcon
Falco mexicanus

The head is squarish in shape with a flat top.

Front view of an adult prairie falcon showing the large, bulbous, dark brown eyes and bright yellow cere.

The long yellow toes of this perched prairie falcon seem to wrap around the branch.

A prairie falcon's white throat and cheek areas are separated by a pronounced brown malar stripe.

When the falcon is partially alarmed the feathers of the nape and shoulders begin to rise.

This photo shows the wide spacing between the legs.

A close-up of the belly shows the random flow of the brown spots and the supple nature of the soft-edged feathers located in this region.

The falcon steps up onto the gloved hand of the author, every feather raised in apparent agitation.

The soft, translucent feathers of the breast contrast strongly with the hard-edged, neat rows of feathers found on the wings.

This interesting pose shows the folding sequence of the major flight feathers and total elevation of the scapular and nape feather groups.

An upright, alert pose showing partially opened wings and flared alula feathers. Note the contrasting silver and white barring found under the wings.

A close-up of the face highlights the delicate directional flow of the whiskerlike rictal bristles in front of and below the eye. Interesting areas can be found where the soft cheek and jaw feathers join the yellow fleshy parts of the bill.

The sharply notched lower mandible locks tightly into the upper mandible when the bill is shut, creating a scissorlike shearing action that easily slices through even the toughest flesh and bone.

This picture reveals the subtle scale patterns of falcon feet. What a contrast to the platelike armor found on the feet of many other diurnal raptors.

Notice the soft, fleshy quality of the feet and the flexibility of the long toes as evidenced by this bird's left inside talon lying flat on a branch.

Curiosity and intelligence are two of the countless qualities that make the prairie falcon such an endearing bird.

An upright position viewed from the back intended to make the prairie falcon look larger and more intimidating.

All the upper tail coverts and rump feathers are visible as the bird drops both wings below the tail.

This falcon appears a bit disheveled because it is molting from immature into adult plumage.

This full-body profile shows a nice folded-wing layout. Also notice the pronounced webbing between the middle and outside toes.

Peregrine Falcon
Falco peregrinus

PERFECTION IN FORM, FLIGHT, AND EVOLUTIONARY function—what more can be said of this amazing creature?

Reputed to be the fastest organism on the planet, the peregrine in a full vertical stoop has been clocked at speeds in excess of 160 miles an hour.

The peregrine falcon inhabits a variety of environments, with nineteen subspecies occurring worldwide. Almost wiped out in North America by the indiscriminate use of DDT, the peregrines have become a symbol of success in recent years as they are beginning to reappear at many long-vacant nesting sites east of the Mississippi. This incredible recovery can be attributed to the long, hard work and dedication of the Peregrine Fund, formerly based at Cornell University, now at the World Center for Birds of Prey in Boise, Idaho.

A medium-sized raptor, the peregrine appears quite dark on its back and head with a heavily barred white and black belly area. Its large, dark eyes are framed by an eyelid of pale yellow. The cere and feet also share this yellow color. Juveniles have eyelids, cere, and feet of pale blue.

Peregrines are easily identifiable due to the dis-tinct dark sideburns that extend down to the chin area. This dark malar stripe is bordered by white cheek feathers. The chest area can vary from pure white to tan and in some subspecies is a beautiful peach color flecked with vertical black markings.

Males and females vary in size but not in coloration. Females are about one-third larger than males and their head shape is generally rounder and lacks the angularity of the smaller males.

A peregrine's diet is comprised mostly of other birds usually caught on the wing. The hunting prowess of peregrines is of mythical proportions; throughout history the peregrine falcon has been the bird of choice among the falconry elite.

The word "peregrine" means traveler or wanderer—an appropriate name for a bird so widely distributed throughout the world. Recently in some cities in the United States and Canada, peregrines have begun nesting on the ledges of tall buildings. This is not surprising when one considers the similarity between these ledges and the high cliffs of many coastal waterways. An overabundance of pigeons and starlings is readily available as an additional enticement.

SPECIES PROFILE

1. Sizes of peregrines range from 16 to 20 inches long, the female being larger.
2. Both sexes have identical markings and coloration.
3. Peregrines have disproportionately large feet with long, slender toes.
4. Distinctive black malar stripes adorn the head.
5. Neck, back, and wing top surfaces are bluish to slate gray in color.
6. Peregrines have a shorter tail in relation to body length than do prairie falcons.
7. The overall body color may vary considerably based on subspecies. The darkest, largest peregrines are of the Pealei group, sometimes referred to as Peale's falcons.
8. The peregrine feeds primarily on other birds.
9. It was once known as the "duck hawk" or "great-footed hawk."
10. It nests on cliffs, rarely builds a nest, and usually lives in close proximity to open water.

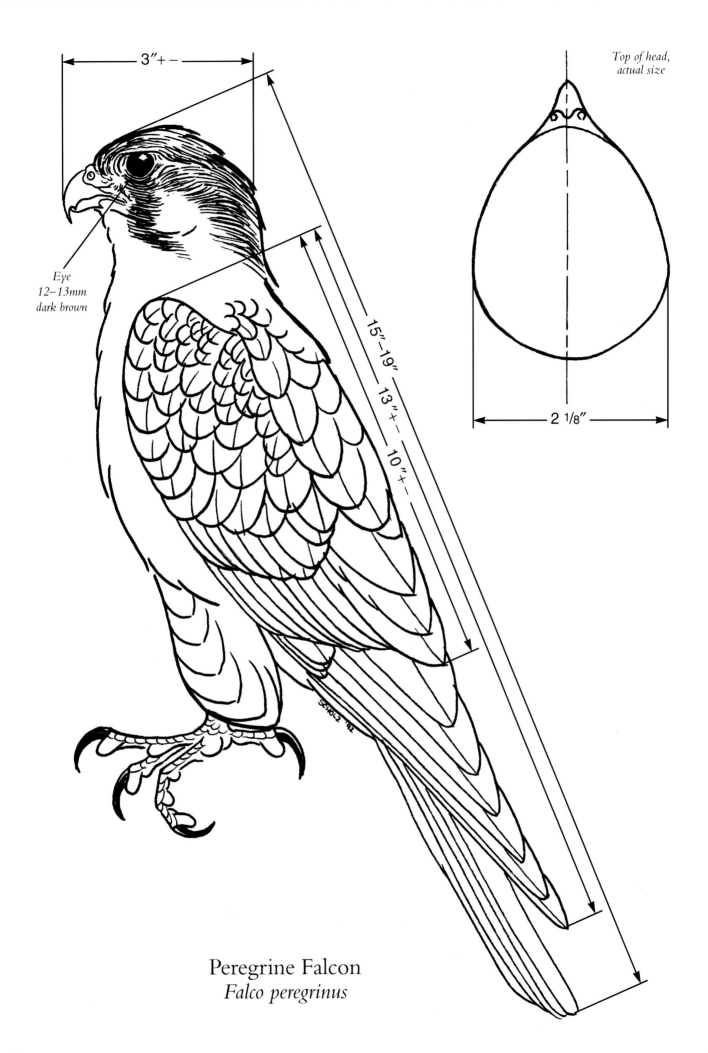

3"+−

Top of head,
actual size

Eye
12−13mm
dark brown

15"−19"

13"+−

10"+−

2 1/8"

SCHOLZ '92

Peregrine Falcon
Falco peregrinus

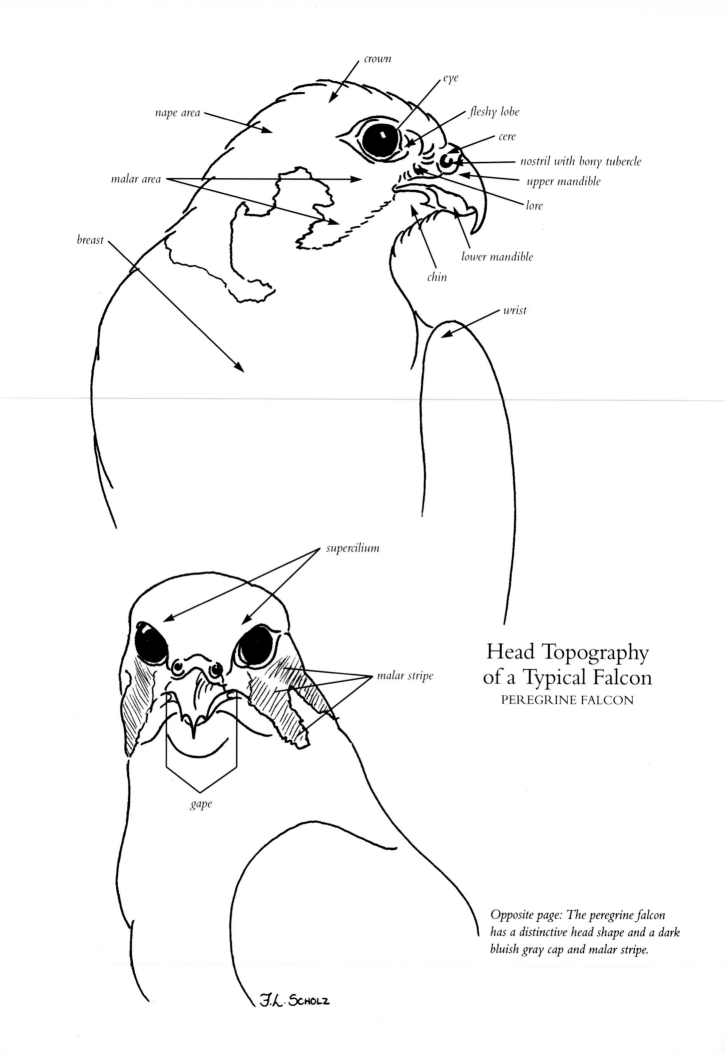

crown

eye

fleshy lobe

cere

nostril with bony tubercle

upper mandible

lore

nape area

malar area

lower mandible

breast

chin

wrist

supercilium

malar stripe

gape

Head Topography of a Typical Falcon
PEREGRINE FALCON

Opposite page: The peregrine falcon has a distinctive head shape and a dark bluish gray cap and malar stripe.

F.L. Scholz

CINDY KILGORE-BROWN

When the mouth is open the soft, fleshy folds of skin at the corners of the mouth expand and flare outward, especially the lower lips. Note the beautiful subtleties of the cere and upper mandible.

Four distinct ridges form the roof of the mouth on most diurnal raptors. This photo shows the coloring and makeup of the roof of this peregrine's mouth.

The scalloped head feathers all seem to flow toward one invisible point at the back of the head. Note how the head feathers turn separately from the underlying breast feathers when the head is turned completely around.

Three separate feather groups are displayed here: the nape, the scapulars, and the upper wing feathers.

The clean, elegant patterns created by the back feathers all complement one another. Note the uneven staggering of the secondary coverts.

Not much goes unnoticed by this ultra-alert raptor looking 180 degrees over its shoulder.

Flowing from around the eyes and onto the sides of the neck, the small, rounded feathers create an interesting pattern of light and dark.

Beautiful light blue and dark blue barring creates a dazzling pattern throughout the back of this peregrine.

As the falcon looks over its shoulder the cream-colored upper breast feathers gently overlap onto the gray-blue feathers of the shoulders and back.

CINDY KILGORE-BROWN

Notice the size, shape, and directional flow of the tiny feathers covering the upper wing area as this curious peregrine looks to the sky.

CINDY KILGORE-BROWN

The lighter-colored feathering of the forehead region is apparent in this photo. The dark malar stripe cuts down directly below the eye and extends well past the jaw line.

CINDY KILGORE-BROWN

The large, dispassionate eye of this tiercel is angled forward, affording the falcon a wide range of vision. Note the sharp downward angle of the lip.

The dark black streaking and barring of the belly and undersides of the wings contrasts sharply with the peach-colored breast feathers and stark white belly and legs. Note the long toes and needle sharp talons.

This three-quarter front view shows the heavily muscled shoulder area and the regimented feather patterns of the upper wing and wrist areas. Note the directional flow of the secondaries as opposed to the primaries.

Opposite page: A nice full-body front view of an adult female peregrine falcon.

This peregrine strikes a defiant pose as it shifts its weight onto its left foot and begins to open its right wing.

Another character pose study. Note the distinct patterns on the tarsus feathers; they are known as "flags" in birders' circles.

Full back view showing the nape, back, scapulars, tertials, and major flight feathers. Pay close attention to feather shape and the way in which the different feather groups overlap one another.

Gyrfalcon
Falco rusticolus

ROYAL, MAJESTIC, AND MAGNIFICENT ARE JUST A FEW colorful adjectives that describe this largest and most northerly member of the falcon family. Occurring in three distinct color phases, the gyrfalcon (pronounced jeerfalcon) prefers to nest along the rough, rocky coasts of the continents and islands of the extreme northern latitudes, where abundant seabirds make up a large part of its diet. Well suited to the frigid north, the gyrfalcon is the only member of the falcon family that can completely cover its toes with its belly feathers when perched. In Elizabethan times it was the white gyrfalcon that was reserved to be owned and flown only by kings and emperors. To this day, tremendous prices are paid by some Middle East falconers for a prime white gyrfalcon, which unfortunately puts heavy pressure on wild nesting birds.

Due to its larger size, the gyrfalcon lacks the maneuverability of its smaller cousins, but it more than makes up for this with its powerful flight. In fact, in a straight-line, level flight pattern a gyrfalcon is much faster than a peregrine. This is why a low-level direct pursuit is a commonly used hunting tactic.

In flight a gyrfalcon's wings look broader and less pointed than do those of the smaller falcons, and it flies with slower, deeper, and more powerful wing beats. The feathering of gyrfalcons appears a bit looser and fluffier than that of peregrines, which is not surprising when you consider where it lives and breeds. The primaries of the folded wings extend down to about one-half the tail length. A gyrfalcon's feet and toes are shorter and heavier in proportion to its body size than those of other falcons and are extremely powerful, allowing it to feed on a variety of prey from lemmings to large arctic hares.

SPECIES PROFILE

1. Its large size—21 to 24 inches—long tail, and massive proportions set the gyrfalcon apart from other falcons.
2. Females are much larger and heavier than males.
3. Its coloring is highly variable, ranging from pure white to deep silvery gray with heavy barring on the tail and wings.
4. The body has a heavy-shouldered appearance tapering back to a long, pointed tail.
5. The powerful notched bill appears large in relation to head size.
6. The body feathers are looser and fluffier than those of other falcons.
7. The leg feathers extend farther down the tarsus toward the foot (a cold weather adaptation).
8. Juvenile birds have a bluish-colored cere, eye ring, and feet.
9. Both juvenile and adult birds have dark brown eyes.
10. The gyrfalcon feeds primarily on other birds, goose size and smaller, but it will also prey on small mammals.

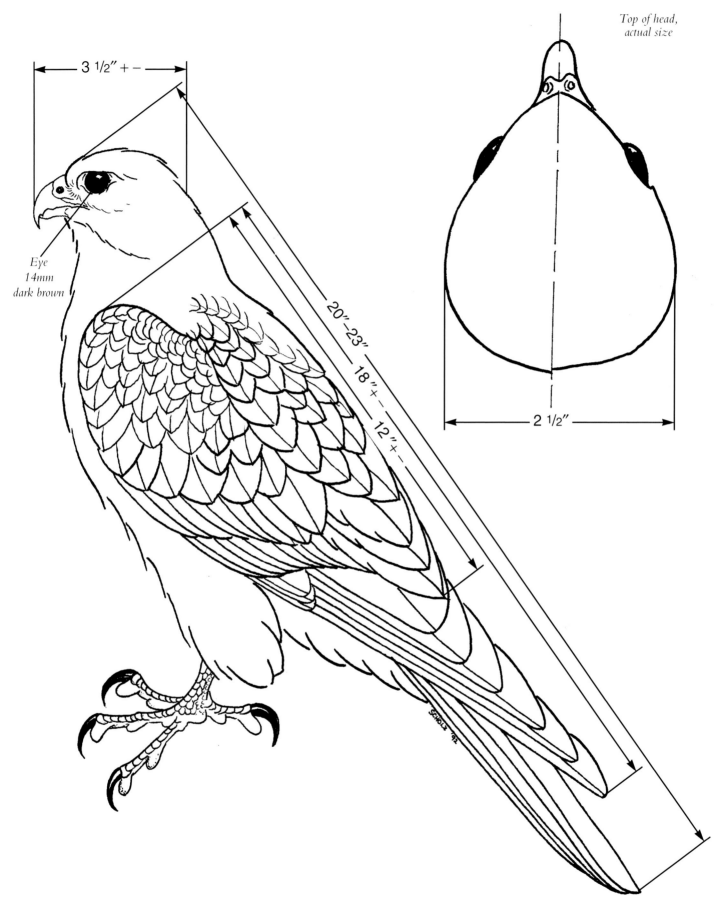

3 ½" + −

Top of head,
actual size

*Eye
14mm
dark brown*

20"-23"

18" + −

12" + −

2 ½"

SCHOLZ '91

Arctic Gyrfalcon
Falco rusticolus

Arctic Gyrfalcon
HEAD STUDIES (ACTUAL SIZE)

A relaxed gyrfalcon's long, hairlike chin feathers hang loosely down from the lower mandible, resembling a small beard.

The back of an adult gyrfalcon showing the elongated, slightly pointed nape, scapulars, and secondary coverts.

The long, slender primaries extend about three-quarters of the total length of the tail and are edged with white on dark-phase and silver-phase gyrfalcons.

On the folded wings the secondary coverts angle down sharply, flowing in a different direction from the secondaries and primaries.

The scale pattern along the toes looks almost reptilian. Notice the pronounced scale at the joint of the outside toe.

The head feathers all converge at the back of the head just above the heavily muscled shoulders.

This gyrfalcon has a slightly square shape to its head, and the feather tracts of the jaw and chin are quite well defined.

The gyrfalcon has shorter, stouter toes and legs in relation to body size than do the peregrine falcon, prairie falcon, and merlin.

The cere appears to be partially covered with very fine feather stubble up to and partly surrounding the nostril. The bony tubercle is visible in the nostril opening.

The various sizes and distinctive shapes and patterns of the upper wing feathers make for an interesting design.

Some falcons develop a series of ridges along each side of the upper mandible that look almost like dual tomial teeth.

An excellent view of leg position and lower mandible detail.

Gyrfalcons have the unique ability to swivel the rear toe, or hallux, around to the front. This is thought to be an adaptation to their harsh, frigid environment.

This full-body side view affords a good look at the long and narrow primary feathers of which nine can be seen.

This interesting close-up shows the feathers of the upper breast area slightly overlapping the wrist of the wing.

Opposite page: A splendid combination of power and beauty, the gyrfalcon is wide at the shoulder and tapers down to the tip of its long, graceful tail.

Gyrfalcons have extremely well-developed webbing between the toes and very fine scale texture on the pads under the toes.

Opposite page: A long, supple neck is essential for a creature so visually dependent. Note the fairly small head in relation to body size.

RED-TAILED
Búteo jamaicénsis

HAWKS
BUTEOS

HARRIS
Parabúteo unicínctus

FERRUGINOUS
Búteo regális

RED-SHOULDERED
Búteo lineátus

REED A. PRESCOTT III

HAWKS
BUTEOS

BROAD-WINGED
Búteo platyperus

ROUGH-LEGGED
Búteo lagópus

REED A. PRESCOTT III

Buteos

THE BUTEOS, OR SOARING HAWKS, ARE SOME OF THE most readily identifiable birds of prey in North America. Often seen circling high overhead, these broad-winged, round-tailed, sharp-eyed predators take advantage of the rising warm air currents in their endless search for a next meal. In the United States and Canada buteos can be found in an incredible range of habitats. Broad-winged hawks and red-shouldered hawks inhabit dense woodlands and mountainous pine forests, while species such as the Harris' hawk and Swainson's hawk prefer more open, desertlike conditions.

Size varies greatly among the North American buteos, ranging from the broad-winged hawk (13 to 17 inches in body length) up to the large, heavy ferruginous hawk (22 to 27 inches long), which is sometimes confused from a distance with a bald or golden eagle.

The word buteo is from Latin and means "buzzard"; in Europe they are still called by this name. Unlike many other species of raptors, members of the buteo genus have been named for their distinct physical characteristics: broad-winged, red-shouldered, red-tailed, rough-legged, and so on.

In general, buteos are not terribly fussy about what they eat. They tend to be less specialized than the accipiters or falcons in terms of acquiring prey and will dine on almost anything they can overcome. Even toads aren't safe from a hungry red-tailed, red-shouldered, or broad-winged hawk.

Nothing rivals the experience of witnessing these superb hunters in action. While banding hawks with my friend Roger Jones in Virginia one sunny October weekend, I felt a sense of what it must be like at the receiving end of a red-tailed hawk stoop. As I followed the circling hawk with my binoculars, Roger tugged at a string connected to a pigeon lure, causing it to flutter up and down. Well concealed in a nearby blind, we had front-row seats to a drama that has been played out over millions of years.

Several thousand feet below, the fluttering pigeon caught the attention of the passing hawk. The lazy circling ceased as the hungry raptor tucked its wings and dropped from the sky. As though guided by an invisible wire, the compact form grew increasingly larger as it rocketed toward its intended target. With long legs extended, the speeding red-tail made last-second adjustments prior to the strike.

A millisecond before clobbering the hopeless pigeon, the perplexed hawk found itself caught in an invisible net barrier watching its meal walk away. We rushed out of the blind and untangled the defiant predator. After recording its weight and measurements and fitting a band to its leg, we admired this fabulous bird. Such physical perfection set free to hunt again.

OPEN WING
TOP VIEW

To take advantage of rising currents of warm air called thermals, buteos have developed a highly specialized wing structure

Note the four heavily-notched outer primaries

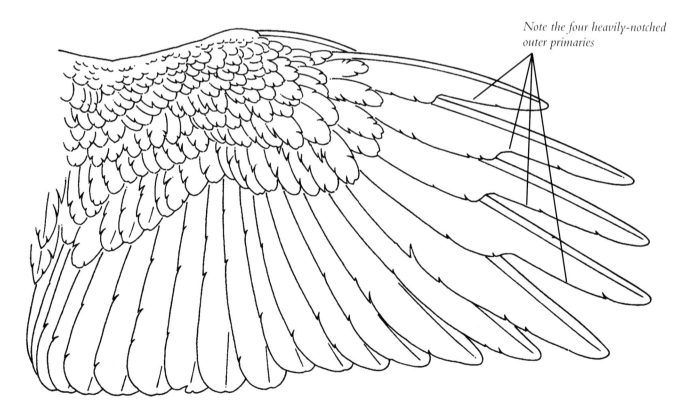

OPEN WING
BOTTOM VIEW

Typical Buteo Wing
Red-tailed Hawk
Buteo jamaicensis

Broad-winged Hawk
Buteo platypterus

SMALLEST OF THE NORTH AMERICAN BUTEOS, THIS stout hawk hardly larger than a crow feeds on a variety of small rodents, reptiles, amphibians, and birds. Broad-winged hawks are quiet, reclusive birds of the deep forest known for their apparent tameness when approached. In these gentle, somewhat sluggish mannerisms it differs greatly from many other raptors, which is why falconers tend to overlook the broad-wing as a hunting companion.

In form and coloration the broad-winged hawk is truly a beautiful bird. Rich rufous brown upper parts, soft white underparts streaked with auburn, and a distinct black and white barred tail all add up to a wonderful collage of subtle colors and patterns. The broad-wing possesses all the classic buteo traits combined in one package—the quintessential hawk.

Fortunately, the broad-winged hawk remains numerous throughout its range. Shy and retiring during late spring and summer when it is occupied with nesting activities, it is rarely seen until a fall phenomenon occurs. Suddenly this inconspicuous raptor becomes one of the most noticeable as thousands gather together to form flocks, or "kettles," that drift lazily southward on their autumnal migration. Broad-wings, the only birds of prey that migrate in flocks, have delighted millions fortunate enough to witness these large rafts of circling migrants as they funnel south along age-old routes. Broad-winged hawks are the only eastern buteos to actually leave the continental United States and winter in Central and South America, where, unfortunately, they are subjected to many more perils than they face in their northern homes. South of the U.S. border, the harmful pesticide DDT is still used by farmers to control insects. Birds are also shot at and trapped more frequently throughout Central and South America, where conservation ethics are not as strong as in the United States.

SPECIES PROFILE

1. The broad-wing's small size, compact shape, short, stubby tail, and broad, rounded wings distinguish it in flight.
2. Body size ranges from 13 to 17 inches long.
3. The sexes are virtually identical, with females being slightly larger.
4. The cere, eyebrow, legs, and feet are pale yellow to flesh colored in juveniles.
5. A soft, chocolate brown eye is achieved after the second year of age.
6. The tail exhibits wide black and white bands—three black, two white.
7. Young broad-wings lack the distinctive tail pattern.
8. The overall back area is rufous brown with a heavily streaked head.
9. The broad-wing is one of the most common woodland hawks.

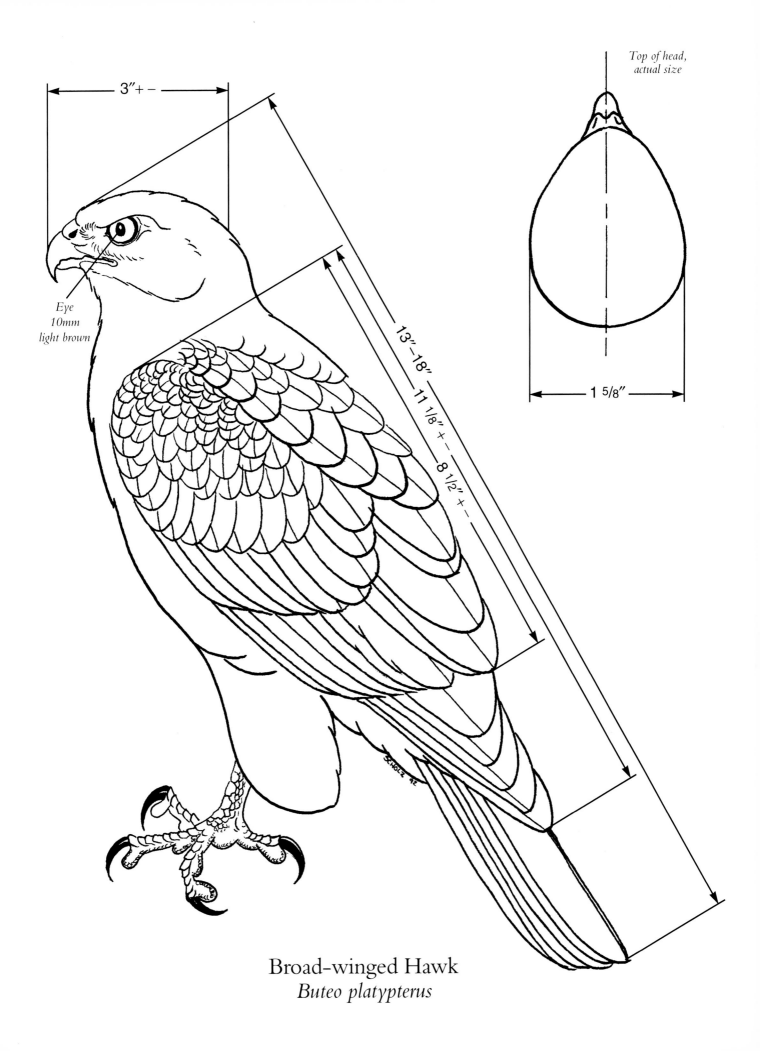

3"+ −

Eye
10mm
light brown

13"–18"

11 ⅛" +−

8 ½" +−

Top of head,
actual size

1 5/8"

SCHOLZ 42

Broad-winged Hawk
Buteo platypterus

The slender bill, soft brown eyes, and cryptic brown coloring make the broad-wing difficult to spot when perched in a stand of trees.

As the scapular feathers cascade down the back they increase in size, becoming much broader at the base.

Opposite page: Smallest of the North American buteos, the broad-winged hawk seems perfectly suited to a life in the deep woodlands.

The tertials, primaries, and tip of the tail are all lightly edged with white.

The undertail coverts are large, soft, and billowy and seem to flow up onto the top of the tail.

Opposite page: This broad-wing strikes a pose that shows off its many shades of brown throughout the back area.

With the primaries dropped the broad dark bands of the tail become apparent, as do the large, well-proportioned tertial feathers covering the rump.

The belly and chest areas are off-white with deep chestnut-colored barring around the legs and belly. Notice the heavy streaking throughout the breast.

The classic buteo form: square at the shoulder, well-proportioned head and feet, and short, rounded tail.

Heavy, broad, platelike scales are found on the front of the legs.

Adult broad-winged hawks have three distinct dark bands across the top of the wide tail.

This rear view reveals the way the large tertial feathers can overlap when the wings are folded.

The interplay of color throughout the chest provides a challenge to even the most highly skilled painters. The feathering in this area is subtle yet vibrant and rich in color.

A noticeable field mark of a flying broad-wing (in addition to its banded tail) is the dark border of the opened wing.

In strong contrast to the stark white underwing is the deep brown upper wing surface. Note the faint barring on the primaries and secondaries.

The heavily scaled feet of the broad-winged hawk enable it to catch a wide variety of prey items.

Top, bottom, and above right: These three photos illustrate the unique locking mechanism of the feet of all raptors. As the leg and foot are drawn up toward the body, the tendons automatically tighten up and cause the foot to lock shut. Also note how the tarsus feathers blend up into the flank feathers and virtually disappear from sight.

Red-shouldered Hawk
Buteo lineatus

THE WIDELY DISTRIBUTED RED-SHOULDERED HAWK is represented by five subspecies throughout the United States and Canada. Red-shouldered hawks get their name from the distinct reddish brown feather patches located at the "shoulder" of the wing on adult birds. Found throughout the East and on the extreme West Coast, red-shoulders are most prevalent in southeastern woodlands and in damp deciduous growths around ponds and lakes. The bird is a patient hunter; an inconspicuous red-shouldered hawk will sit for hours scanning the forest floor from a high perch waiting for a small creature to reveal itself. A list of its prey includes a broad spectrum of squirrel-sized and smaller animals ranging from beetles and snakes to birds, mammals, and even fish.

Visually there is little difference between the sexes, and both birds share in the feeding and raising of young. Heavily barred major flight and tail feathers along with the reddish shoulder feathers help to distinguish this medium-sized buteo from its slightly larger and heavier cousin the red-tailed hawk.

Flight characteristics are unique: the red-shouldered hawk has a much busier flapping flight and soars in much tighter circles than most other similar-sized buteos.

One of the more vocal hawks, the red-shoulder is often heard before it is seen, its piercing "kee-yer, key-ah-yer" cries penetrating the solitude of the field and forest and inspiring such mimics as the blue jay to join in the chorus.

SPECIES PROFILE

1. The red-shoulder is a large to midsized mottled brown hawk with black and white barred wings and tail.
2. Its size varies from 16 to 20 inches.
3. The sexes are alike, although the female may be slightly larger.
4. The overall body appearance is more slender and streamlined than that of other similarly sized buteos.
5. Red-shouldered hawks vary widely in breast and belly coloration from brick red to a washed-out, pale orange.
6. The eye color is a warm, dark brown; the eye lenses look a bit bulbous.
7. The cere, legs, and feet are pale yellow.
8. The legs and toes appear smaller and less powerful than those of a red-tail.
9. Red-shoulders have a unique habit of decorating their nests with bits of green foliage.
10. They frequently feed on snakes and amphibians.

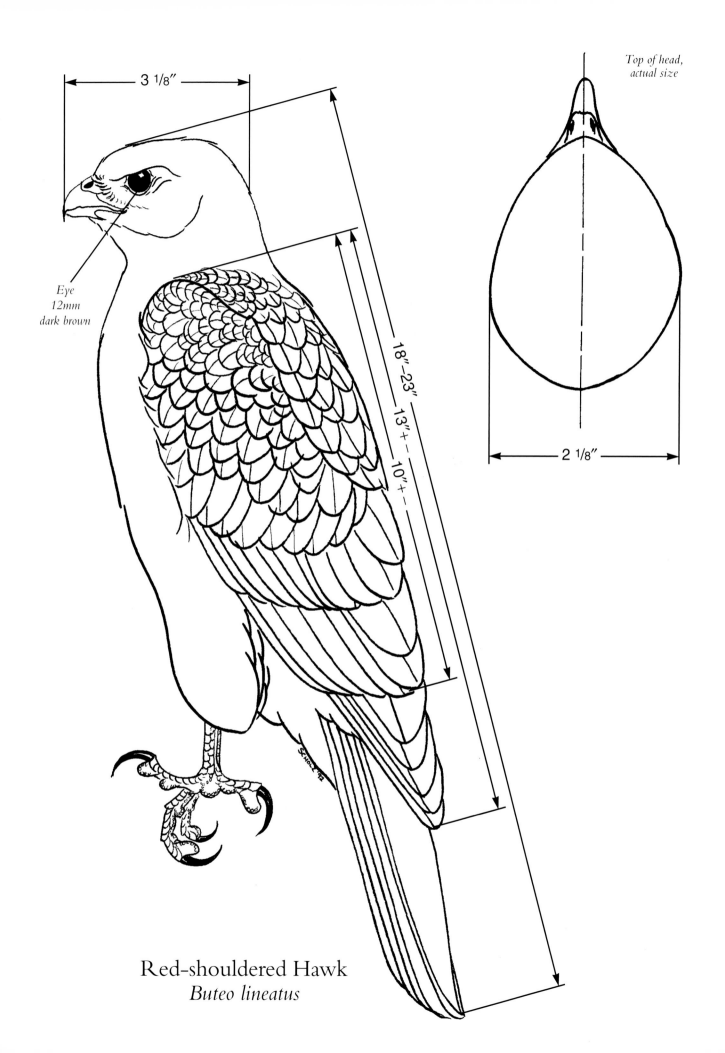

3 1/8"

Eye
12mm
dark brown

18"–23"

13"+–

10"+–

Top of head,
actual size

2 1/8"

Red-shouldered Hawk
Buteo lineatus

A small brown eye and small narrow bill are two of the distinguishing characteristics of the red-shouldered hawk.

The dark, heavily banded tail is a distinct field mark.

The soft, broad streaks establish the feather flow around the eye and onto the back. Note the subtle transition of color where the chin meets the upper breast area.

The many shades of brown found throughout the back area create a beautiful mottled appearance. This bird is also going through a heavy molt, which accounts for the untidy appearance of the feathers.

When a red-shoulder is alarmed, the long nape feathers and the feathers on the back of the head become erect, giving the head a fierce wedge shape.

An alarmed red-shoulder viewed from the front.

The upper wing coverts of the underside of the wing are brick red, contrasting sharply with the stark black and white barring of the major flight feathers.

The dark tail bars, primaries, and primary coverts gradually fade to a softer brown closer to the body.

A close-up of the distinct white spots found on the secondaries of a red-shouldered hawk.

A red-shoulder's feet are quite small but heavily scaled, most likely an adaptation for catching its preferred reptilian prey.

Often seen perched out on the springy limbs of saplings, red-shoulders will wait patiently until a prey item is spotted and then drop down to subdue it.

Above and right: A very terrestrial hunter, the red-shouldered hawk often shuffles along swampy areas hoping to stir up a possible meal. Rodents, reptiles, and amphibians figure into the diet of this long-legged hunter. Note how well the red-shouldered hawk blends into its surroundings.

JACK MURRAY

JACK MURRAY

Breast color varies tremendously on red-shouldered hawks. Generally, the farther south they are found, the paler the red coloring. A western race known as the California red-shoulder has bright brick red belly and breast feathers.

A close-up of the back of the head and nape showing the cascading mottled feathers found in this region.

This photo highlights the triangular head shape of this gorgeous midsized raptor.

Harris' Hawk
Parabuteo unicinctus

MY FIRST PERSONAL ENCOUNTER WITH THE HARRIS' Hawk was several years ago on Long Island, New York, where a falconer friend, Brian Hyland, was exhibiting his beautiful Harris' at a bird carving show. Having known of these hawks only from pictures, I was taken aback by its exquisite form and coloration—it looked somewhat like a small, long-legged, slender golden eagle.

Harris' hawks are named after Edward Harris, who was a close friend and companion of John James Audubon. They are found in the arid southwestern part of the United States and in Mexico. A particular favorite of falconers, this fine bird is a most capable hunter whose prey selection ranges from large desert hares to various birds, reptiles, and rodents.

Unlike other birds of prey, Harris' hawks have a highly developed social order and often hunt in groups. While one or two birds flush out the quarry, others perch in wait ready to attack the fleeing victim. But to the victor go the spoils—once the prey is subdued, it is fiercely guarded and seldom shared among the others!

Harris' hawks are easily recognizable in adult plumage by their dark brown coloring, bright rufous red wing coverts and thighs, and long, dark tail sprouting from a pure white rump and terminating with a white tip. A large, round, brown eye framed by a heavy brow gives this bird a no-nonsense appearance. The cere, legs, and feet are yellow. Perhaps due to its terrestrial hunting tactics or its habit of perching on cacti, Harris' hawks have well-developed, very long exposed legs, which give them a storklike appearance quite distinctive for a North American buteo.

SPECIES PROFILE

1. The Harris' is a moderate to large-sized (19- to 22-inch) dark brown hawk.
2. It has a slender build with a long, white-tipped tail.
3. A predominantly yellow cere and lore frame the dark brown eye.
4. The yellow legs are disproportionately long with well-developed, powerful toes.
5. The sexes are alike in color and size.
6. The upper wing coverts and tarsus feathers show bright rufous coloring.
7. Tight, compact feathering amplifies the trim lines of this sleek bird.
8. The sharply hooked bill is light powder blue at the base, gradually tapering to a deep blue-black tip.
9. The short primaries extend just one-quarter of the way down the tail with the wings folded.
10. Harris' hawks sometimes hunt in cooperative groups of five or more birds.

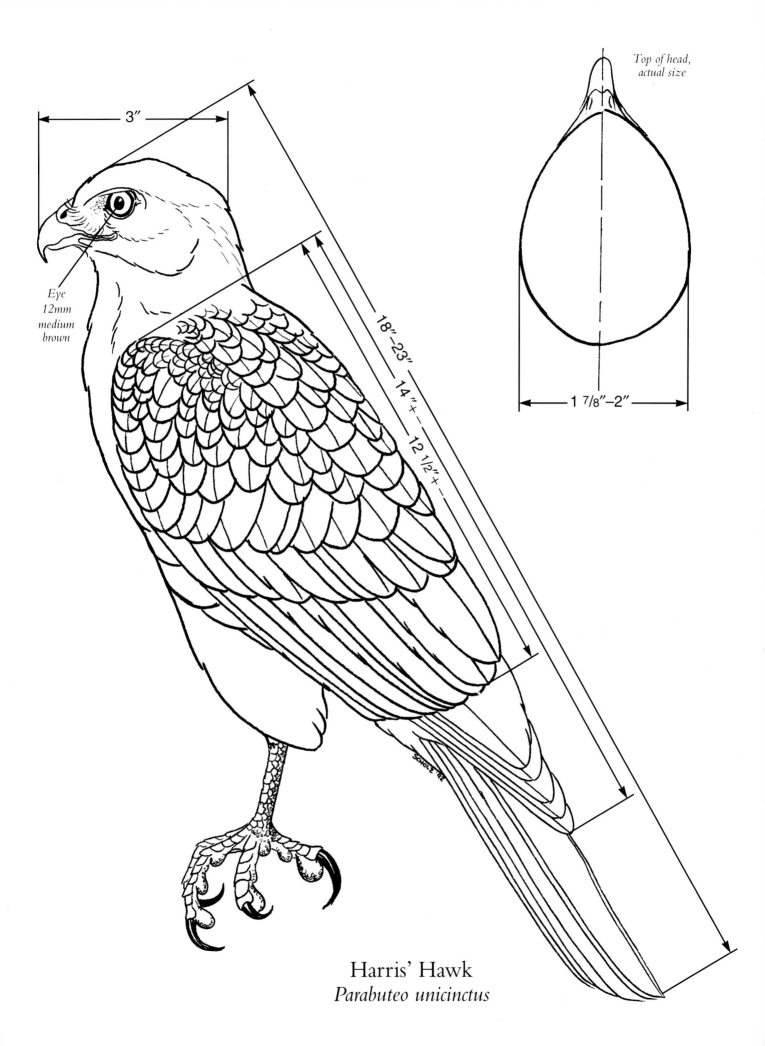

3″

Eye
12mm
medium
brown

18″–23″

14″+–

12 1/2″+–

Top of head,
actual size

1 7/8″–2″

Harris' Hawk
Parabuteo unicinctus

The underside of the throat and lower mandible. Note the patterns of the various feather groups.

This close-up shows the tight, clean lines of an adult Harris' hawk's face. The well-proportioned bill and warm brown eye are framed with soft yellow.

This photo illustrates the beautiful feather patterns and gradual transition from dark brown to rich sienna on the upper wings.

Harris' hawks have very long and broad secondaries as shown in this detail of the right wing secondaries and secondary coverts.

Opposite page: Upper wrist area and head profile of an adult female Harris' hawk.

Look at the intensity of the eyes! As the photographer was preparing to shoot this photo, I dangled a dead mouse just above the lens of the camera, and the whole attitude of the hawk changed as if it had been electrically charged.

Note the design and placement of the scales on this left foot. Most buteos share this scale configuration. Also clearly shown is the web connecting the outer toe to the middle toe.

The long, broad tail fathers aid in maneuverability. This bird is molting in a new tail feather.

This puffed-up Harris' hawk is about to settle down and perch comfortably after rousing.

This action is known as rousing; it enables the bird to rearrange and reorganize all its feathers. It may also aid in trapping warm air close to the body for insulation while at rest.

Note the interaction where the two major wing feather groups come together on the back.

The heavily muscled and well-feathered back of the head and nape.

Full body back view showing the characteristic long, wide tail, short primaries, and long, broad secondary feathers.

This side profile shows the incredibly well-proportioned, streamlined shape of the Harris' hawk.

Above and opposite page: As the hawk assumes a more upright pose, note how the center of balance shifts forward.

Feather shape and size change drastically from the ear coverts to the nape and shoulder regions.

The heavily scaled feet and toes, along with very long legs, allow the Harris' hawk to perch on the many cactus plants that thrive in the arid southwestern United States.

Harris' hawks have a distinct white undertail covert area.

Note the flow of the rictal bristles from the lore area onto the cere of this adult female.

Note the subtle differences between the head of this adult male Harris' hawk and that of the female. The male's eyes seem smaller in relation to head size, as does the bill.

The layered feather design of the undertail coverts is evident in this photo.

The white undertail coverts seem to billow up and around the tail feathers. Note the position of the outer toe and talon of this hawk's left foot.

Much can be learned of the nature of foot design by carefully studying this picture. Note the differences in talon size and toe thickness.

A very common way of perching for many raptors is to tuck one foot up into the belly feathers.

Looking as much like a teddy bear as a hawk, this little male assumes a relaxed pose. The details around the eyelid are visible in this photo. The hawk seems to have a slightly smiling expression.

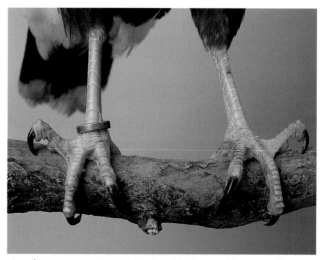

Another common toe position is with the outside toes arcing up. This looks very dramatic on a posed bird.

The ear coverts around the cheek area stand out as a group. Note how they seem to frame the face.

The wide "tough guy" stance and beautifully scalloped chest feathers are just two of the many fine qualities of this elegant bird.

Red-tailed Hawk
Buteo jamaicensis

THE RED-TAILED HAWK HAS BEEN ROUTINELY CURSED at and blasted out of the sky. Irate farmers of years ago ignorantly looked upon the red-tail as the enemy. If they had only known that by virtue of their misplaced anger they were in fact helping out their real enemies, the rats and varmints so destructive to the cycle of life on a farm.

Fortunately for the hawks, human attitudes have taken an about-face from resentment to respect and admiration.

The red-tailed hawk is without question the most far-ranging and recognizable large hawk in the United States and Canada. So varied in coloration is the red-tailed hawk that twelve official subspecies are listed, and many varieties of color phases, or "morphs," are found within each subspecies. Many morphs don't even have red tails!

These large, square-shouldered raptors bear many identifiable field marks. Aside from a brownish red tail, they can also wear a distinct dark brown belly band, or "cummerbund," that horizontally divides the yellow-beige underparts. The amount of brown feathering on the chest and belly area varies tremendously from bird to bird. The Eastern red-tail *(Buteo jamaicensis borealis)* in "classic" coloration has a dark chestnut-colored head and neck graduating to a more rufous brown back and upper wing area. The secondaries and primaries are dark brown with light gray barring gradually shading to solid brownish black at the primary tips. When folded the wings extend about halfway down the length of the tail. Eye color darkens to deep brown usually after the second year of life; juveniles have lighter brownish gray eye coloration.

In the endless quest for food, red-tailed hawks employ many hunting techniques. They perch patiently for hours watching and listening for some unwary small creature to appear, or spiral upward in lazy circles, riding invisible elevators of warm air known as thermals, and scanning open meadows and roadsides for the slightest movement.

Often while hiking the mountains around my home in Vermont, I've watched in awe as these marvelous acrobats wheel across the sky, feeling perhaps a bit sad that I stand unable to join them in their lofty celebration of freedom.

SPECIES PROFILE

1. This large, rugged-looking buteo averages 19 to 24 inches in length.
2. Females are up to 25 percent larger than males.
3. The red-tail is the most recognizable large hawk and is the most widely distributed of all diurnal birds of prey. It is often seen perched along highways or circling lazily overhead.
4. It is highly variable in plumage coloration, from light auburn to deep brown. Totally dark species with red tails are more common in the West.
5. On eastern species the tail is distinctly rust-colored above with occasional barring. Juvenile birds have heavily barred tails and streaked underparts.
6. The eye color changes from light yellowish gray in immatures to dark brown in adults.
7. The cere, legs, and feet on adult birds are yellow.
8. The light buff underparts are divided by a swath of dark feathers across the belly.
9. Powerful stocky feet and toes help the red-tail subdue a wide range of prey.

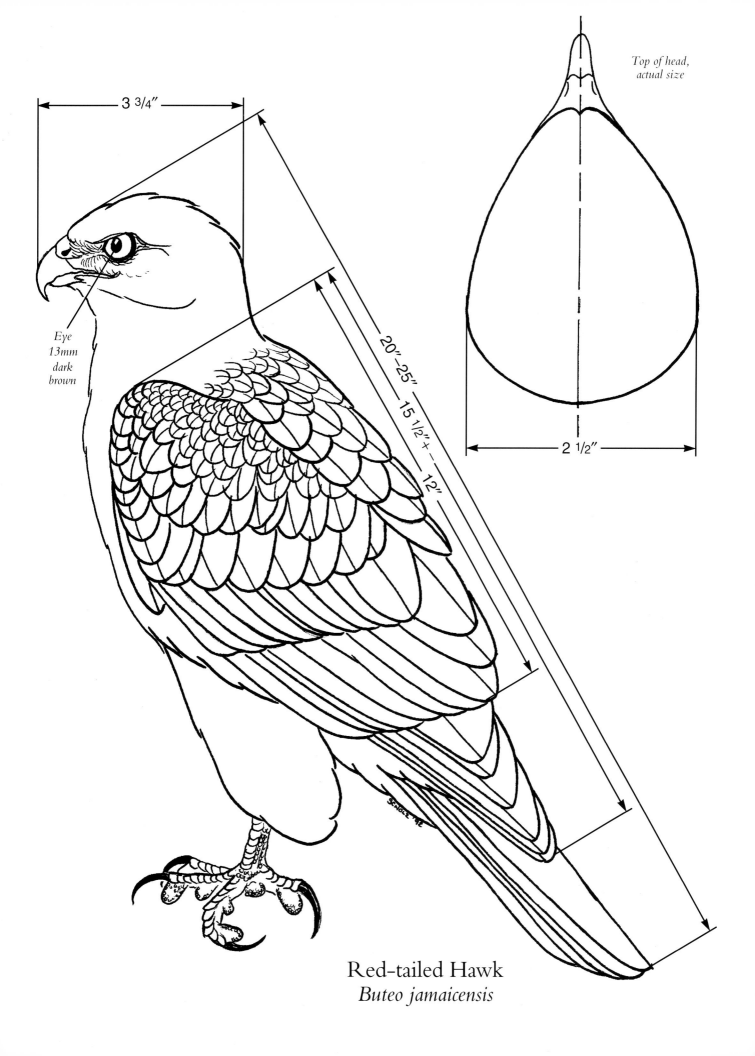

3 3/4″

20″-25″

15 1/2″+ –

12″

Eye
13mm
dark
brown

*Top of head,
actual size*

2 1/2″

Red-tailed Hawk
Buteo jamaicensis

Head profile of an excited adult red-tailed hawk. Note the density of the rictal bristles in front of the eye.

The eye structure is unique: the pupil has a dark ring completely encircling it. Red-tails have eyesight up to eight times more powerful than that of humans.

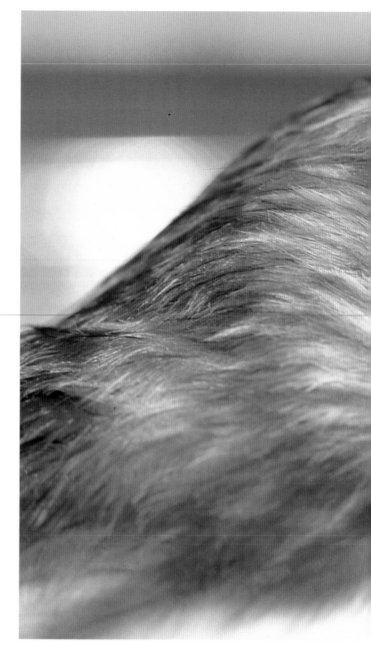

FLOYD SCHOLZ

An adult female red-tail. The dark brown eye is acquired after the bird's second year of life. Note the graceful flow of feathers below and around the eye. The beautiful blue translucency of the bill is also visible.

FLOYD SCHOLZ

Front view showing the directional feather flow up from the cere and forehead area. Note the eyelid and how it converges at the front of the eye.

The point of wing insertion often causes a "traffic jam" of various feather groups. Note how the shoulder tracts and the flank feathers gently flow around the wing.

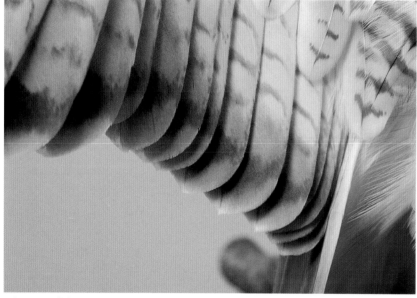

Close-up of the underside section of the secondary feathers showing the subtle blending of colors that occurs here.

The upper chest is one area that can vary tremendously between the races of red-tailed hawks. Some are pure white and some are dark solid brown.

A close-up of the silvery underwing feathers. Note the faint brownish gray barring on the primaries and secondaries.

A three-quarter back view of an adult red-tail showing how the partially spread primaries overlap the tail. Note the extended alula feathers.

Partially spread wing and exposed tail area. The upper tail coverts are a light cream color.

An even closer look at the primary feather groups.

Opposite page: The full back feather layout of an adult red-tailed hawk. Note how the tertials appear to be much lighter in color than the surrounding secondaries and scapular feathers.

This red-tailed hawk strikes a dramatic upright threat pose.

The back of the head seems to flare way out as this red-tailed hawk quickly looks back. Note the strong angle of the leg and how it carries up into the body.

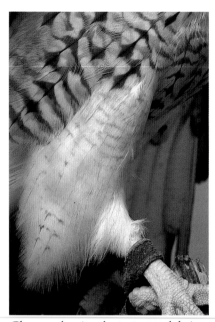

Close-up showing the texture and design of the tarsus feathers.

The soft, furlike tarsus feathers, or "flags," slide out from under the heavily barred flank feathers. Note the thick leg and stout, heavily scaled toes tipped with daggerlike talons.

What a beautiful, rich combination of color and form.

FLOYD SCHOLZ

FLOYD SCHOLZ

An adult Eastern red-tail viewed against its element, the vast blue sky.

Three-quarter rear view of an Eastern red-tail. The complex plumage coloration and feather tract layouts of the wing and back are in full view.

The "classic" red-tailed hawk pose, proud and independent.

The fully extended upper wing surface shows the heavily barred major flight feathers.

The underside of a red-tail wing at full extension. Note the subtle flecking of rust-colored feathers on the wrist area and the heavily notched shape of the first four primaries.

The author studying the subtle complexities of an adult red-tailed hawk. The hawk seems to be engaging in some sort of conversation. Note the sharply hooked upper mandible.

Frontal view of a red-tail striking a defiant pose. The wide leg spacing and distinct belly band of dark brown feathers are clearly visible.

This red-tailed hawk shifts its weight onto its left leg as it rears back in a threatening gesture. Note how the tarsus feathers of the left leg seem to be enveloped into the belly as the weight is placed on it.

Rough-legged Hawk
Buteo lagopus

ONE OF NORTH AMERICA'S LARGEST AND MOST IMpressive hawks, the rough-legged hawk inhabits the cold, rugged terrain north of the tree line of North America and Eurasia. Rivaling the red-tail in terms of color variation, the rough-legged hawk is sometimes described as occurring in two distinct color phases, although in reality such a broad spectrum of shades exists it would be fruitless to try to separate it into two morphs.

Upon close observation, certain physical distinctions become apparent. Rough-legged hawks have very small feet in relation to body size. Also note how the tarsus feathers almost completely cover the legs (the back of the leg is exposed) all the way down to the toes. Birds with this characteristic are called "booted." (It is probably an adaptation to a harsh, frigid environment.) The relatively small head, small, narrow, sharply hooked bill, and ex-

ceptionally large, round eye give this hawk a less fierce appearance.

Kestrel-like in its ability to hover over one area, the rough-legged hawk has long, broad wings and a tail longer than that of most other North American buteos. It is recognizable in flight by these characteristics. In addition, the wings when viewed from below show distinct black "wrist patches."

The rough-leg's diet consists almost exclusively of small rodents that share its habitat. Voles, lemmings, and hares make up a large part of its daily fare.

Well designed for survival in such a barren, cold environment, the rough-legged hawk seems to have been spared from the mindless destruction dealt upon its more southerly cousins by its only real threat—the human race.

SPECIES PROFILE

1. At 19 to 26 inches, the rough-leg is one of the largest North American hawks. The sexes are identical.
2. Rough-legged hawks occur in a wide range of color variations.
3. The small, sharp bill and large, round eyes make the head appear large.
4. Densely feathered "booted" legs account for this hawk's name.
5. The bill is dark blue all the way up to the cere.
6. The cere is pale yellow, and the nostril is quite elliptical in shape.
7. In flight the bright white rump patch is evident.
8. This large hawk has the ability to hover over one area in search of small prey.
9. Its extremely small, feeble feet are suited for its rodent quarry.
10. Well adapted to a harsh, treeless environment, rough-legged hawks nest either on the ground, in trees, or in rocky cliffs.

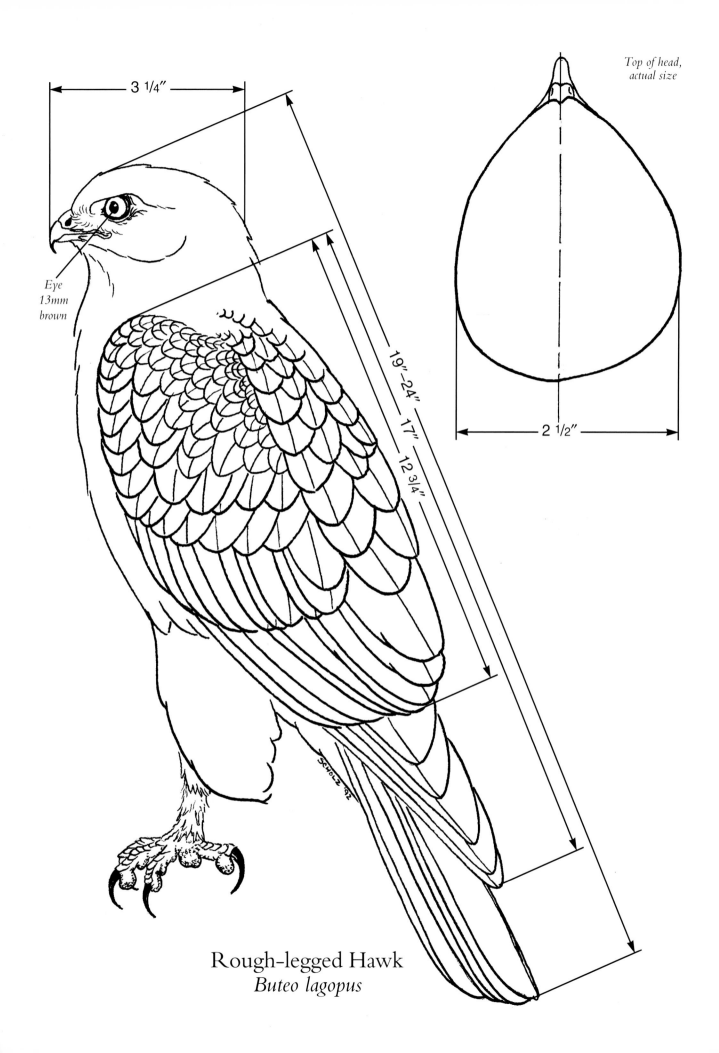

3 1/4"

Eye
13mm
brown

19"-24"

17"

12 3/4"

Top of head,
actual size

2 1/2"

Rough-legged Hawk
Buteo lagopus

Side profile of a light-phase rough-legged hawk. This hawk has a surprisingly small bill in relation to its large head size.

The upper breast is blotched with dark streaks trailing down onto the belly in no particular order or pattern.

As the mouth opens, the tightly pinched corners of the mouth expand to a wide gape, enabling the rough-leg to swallow much of its prey whole.

The intense brown eye is very similar in structure to that of the red-tailed hawk. Note the distinct dark ring around the pupil.

Striking patterns are formed as the feathers flow around the eyes and over the top of the head.

The proportionately small feet of the rough-legged hawk are tipped with needle sharp talons. The legs are heavily feathered all the way down to the tops of the toes, giving this bird its name.

Upper body close-up of an adult light-phase rough-legged hawk.

A three-quarter front view showing the full length of the heavily feathered legs.

The alula feathers of the left wing are partially extended as the large rough-legged hawk prepares to spread its wings.

Opposite page: The large, dense contour feathers of the body aid in insulating the rough-legged hawk against the harsh, cold tundra of its northern home.

The long tail and primaries aid in its hunting technique of flying slowly and sometimes hovering over barren ground in search of lemmings and occasional rabbits.

Fully extended wing underside of a dark-phase rough-legged hawk. The distinct dark "wrist spot" is plainly visible. These wrist spots are an important field identification mark.

The long primaries and relatively narrow wing are adaptations for its method of hunting in the barren arctic landscape.

Ferruginous Hawk
Buteo regalis

WE RAPTOR LOVERS FROM THE EAST SADLY HAVE little or no opportunity to observe this magnificent master of the skies in action. Indigenous to the western half of the United States, the "ferrug," as it is known, is a raptor of vast open spaces and often perches on the ground in search of its small, furry prey. Prairie dogs, ground squirrels, and desert rats figure prominently in its diet, although large desert hares and jackrabbits don't rest when a hungry ferrug is on the prowl.

In researching ferruginous hawks for this book, I have come to respect and admire this fine raptor. Many who know the bird feel it probably is more closely related to the golden eagle than to its smaller buteo cousins. Like the golden eagle, this raptor constructs an enormous stick nest and adds to it every season, usually in a location that affords a commanding view of its domain.

Upon first inspection, distinct features are the wide gape, or corners of the mouth, and the pronounced "leggings"—densely packed tarsus feathers that cover the legs all the way down to the top of the feet. Light-phase ferruginous hawks are immaculately white underneath except for some faint streaking. While the bird is in flight, the dark legs form a distinctive V pattern when viewed from below. The top and back of the head and the neck and back areas are cinnamon red in color, graduating to darker brown primaries, which overlap a pale upper tail surface. The sexes are similar in size and coloration, and it is the female that spends the majority of time at the nest while raising the young.

Recognized as the largest of all the North American buteos, the ferruginous hawk is truly worthy of its Latin name, which means "royal hawk."

═══════════════ SPECIES PROFILE ═══════════════

1. At 23 to 27 inches long, this is the largest and heaviest of all North American hawks.
2. The sexes are identical in size and color.
3. Dense feathers cover the legs and the tops of the feet.
4. The corners of the mouth (gape) are extremely wide.
5. The cere and feet are a deep yellow.
6. The feet, although fairly small in relation to its great size, are extremely powerful.
7. The body is a cinnamon color above, white below.
8. The light brown eyes are framed by yellow eyelids.
9. The ferruginous hawk lives in the western prairies and semiarid plains of the Southwest.

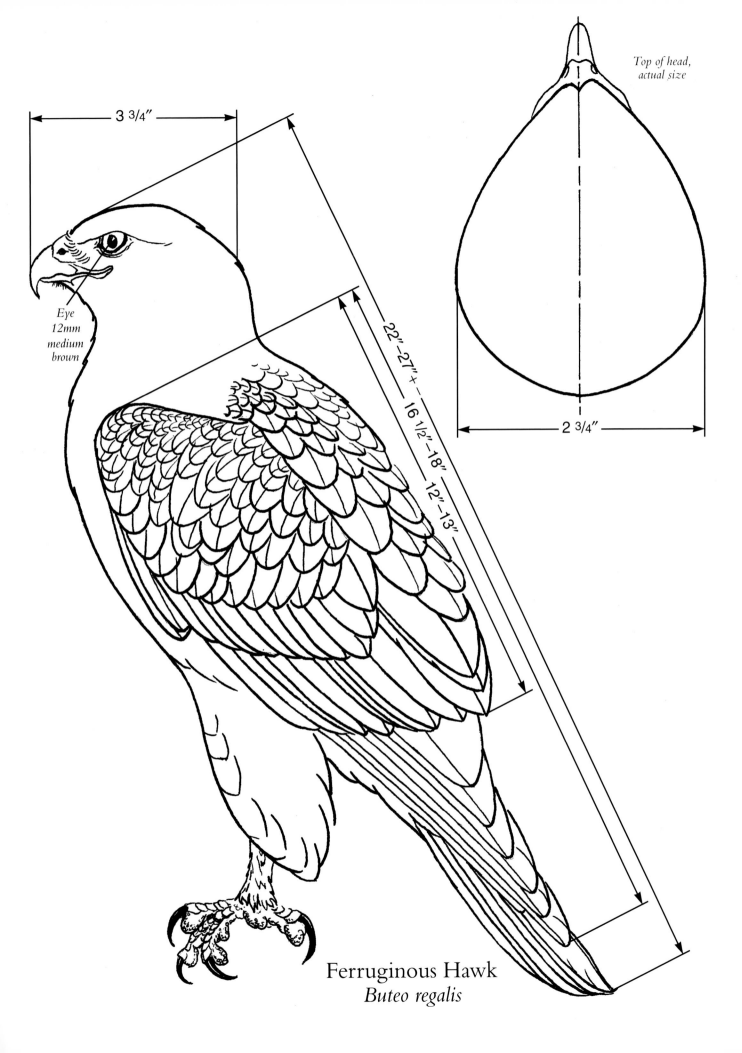

3 3/4"

Eye
12mm
medium
brown

22"-27"+

16 1/2"-18"

12"-13"

Top of head,
actual size

2 3/4"

Ferruginous Hawk
Buteo regalis

This head close-up shows the ferruginous hawk's distinct head shape and wide gape below the eyes.

Opposite page: Head and shoulder profile showing the exquisitely proportioned head-to-bill relationship.

The well-orchestrated feather flow originates from the bill and cere area and flows uniformly up and around the eyes and head.

This hawk is looking sharply down at its talons, which creates a cascading effect on the back of the head and down onto the back.

A low crouch pose amplifies the flatness of the top of the head.

The spear-shaped nape feathers resemble armor plates.

The rich chestnut coloring of the upper shoulder feathers is accented by dark brown streaks through the center of each feather.

The thickly feathered leg is a much darker color than the surrounding belly and flank feathers.

The soft coloring and dense structure of the breast feathers creates an interesting pattern.

The scapular feathers fall into neat rows as they flow over the wing area. Note the hairlike edges of each individual feather.

Notice the pointed tertials and secondaries, the narrow primaries, and the muted colors of the upper tail surface.

An extreme close-up of the shoulder area reveals the small size and compact nature of this feather group.

Close-up of the primary feathers. The white feather shafts gradually shift position toward the center of the feather as the feathers become shorter.

The size difference is remarkable between the inside talon and the middle talon.

The long, broad tail is fully exposed in this photo.

The look that lemmings' nightmares are made of. The beautiful brown eyes appear to be framed by the yellow lips and heavy brow.

The protruding lower lip accentuates the strong recurve of the bill. The jaw line creates an interesting separation between head and chest.

Opposite page: A mantling ferruginous hawk as viewed from the side, with the elevated scapulars shelving out over the tertials and secondaries.

Full back view showing all the major feather groups.

Opposite page: The ferruginous hawk is the largest and widest of all North American buteos. The stout, powerful feet seem disproportionately small in relation to body size.

GOLDEN
EAGLE
Áquila
chrysáetos

BALD
EAGLE
Haliaéetus
leucocéphalus

REED A. PRESCOTT III

EAGLES

Eagles

Until one has actually witnessed a soaring eagle riding the wind, words like sovereignty and majesty remain just meaningless words. It's hard to imagine not feeling moved in some way when standing before such genuine royalty.

From the oldest civilizations we have evidence of the mighty eagle being celebrated, often elevated to godlike status. In one form or another the eagle has always been revered as a symbolic icon, instilling confidence and invincibility in the armies most closely associated with its image of power and conviction.

In today's society, this symbolism still persists in a variety of forms. Our currency, the names we give to our fastest and most formidable war machines, even the symbol of our nation (albeit a gross caricature) features an eagle. Unfortunately for the eagle, humans have bestowed a tremendous amount of excess baggage on a creature that craves solitude and asks only to be left alone.

In North America, the worldwide family of eagles is represented by two species, the American bald eagle and the golden eagle. Although both are called eagles, these large, powerful, flesh-eating birds are not as closely related as one would think. The bald eagle belongs to the order of sea eagles. (Its Latin name, *Haliaeetus leucocephalus*, derived from the Greek *haliatos*, "sea eagle," *leukos*, "white," and *kephale*, "head," affords a fairly graphic description of this bird.) The golden eagle belongs to the order of "booted eagles," regarded as "the most highly evolved of all the birds of prey with the possible exception of the larger falcons" according to Brown and Amadon (Country Life Books, 1968). In fact, based on the taxonomic evolutionary tree, golden eagles are more closely related to the buteos than to the bald eagles they resemble so closely in size and shape.

These two eagles also exhibit striking differences in form. The head and bill differ markedly in size and shape. The bald eagle has a much longer and more bulbous bill profile than the golden eagle. The cere extends close to one-half the overall length, and both the cere and the upper and lower mandibles are uniformly yellow in color. Sleeker and more buteonine in design, the golden eagle's head-to-bill relationship is better proportioned. The top of its bill is dark blue, which graduates to light blue-gray where it meets the pale yellow cere.

The flecked, muted yellow eye of the adult bald eagle contrasts strongly with the dark brown eye of the adult golden eagle. Look closely at the legs and feet of the two species and you'll notice special adaptations. Golden eagles have densely feathered legs, with the feathering extending down to the tops of their toes, and the scales on the bald eagle's feet have a more reticulated pattern.

Although their food preferences do overlap, both birds are superbly designed to exploit the prey species available to them in their respective environments—for bald eagles fish, for golden eagles rabbits and small mammals.

American Bald Eagle
Haliaeetus leucocephalus

THE AMERICAN BALD EAGLE IS THE MOST RECOGNIZable, most often portrayed and, sadly, the most caricatured of all the bird species. In North America we are bombarded by its image. We all carry pictures of bald eagles around with us every day. Just look in your wallet and you'll undoubtedly wish you had a lot more eagle pictures!

Despite all this exposure, very few people know what bald eagles really look like. Much has been written of Benjamin Franklin's protest of the bald eagle as the choice for our national symbol. Franklin placed more emphasis on the eagle's piracy and scavenging habits than on its physical attributes, but at the time, visual symbolism was much more relevant to a young nation than a working knowledge of ornithology.

Whether perched or in flight, adult bald eagles can be quickly identified by their large size, brown body and wings, and white head and tail. Young bald eagles (five years of age and younger) can be easily mistaken for golden eagles due to their lack of the identifiable white parts. Body size is variable depending on geographic location; the southern race is usually smaller and lighter in color than the northern race. Sizes range between 28 and 38 inches with a wingspan averaging 75 to 80 inches.

(These physical dimensions have often been greatly exaggerated. Reports of 9- to 10-foot wingspans are simply not true. The longest documented wingspan of any bald eagle to date stands at about 90 inches, or 7½ feet.)

The female is the larger and heavier of the two sexes and upon close inspection has a slightly larger bill in relation to head size. In adult plumage, the bill, cere, lore, eyelid, legs, and feet are a pale yellow.

While certainly able to catch and overcome a wide variety of prey, bald eagles prefer to feed on the most easily obtainable meal. Dying and dead fish make up a large part of its diet, and it is not above stealing a meal from a smaller eagle or osprey, further adding to the bald eagle's reputation as a scavenger and thief.

Not usually found far from open water or rivers, bald eagles can congregate by the hundreds when the pickings are easy. As the salmon toil their way upstream to spawn they become a source of food for flesh-eating animals large and small, feathered and furred. At times like this in parts of Alaska, bald eagles fly in from hundreds of miles away, assembling in huge numbers to feast on this abundant fare. Such a gathering of these magnificent birds is a truly wondrous spectacle.

SPECIES PROFILE

1. In adult plumage, the bald eagle is the only huge, dark brown bird with a white head and tail. (The white head and tail are attained after the fifth year.)
2. Bald eagle sizes range from 28 to 38 inches with a 6- to 7-foot wingspan. Females are larger and heavier than males.
3. Bill, cere, leg, and foot color ranges from pale to bright yellow.
4. The lower half of the leg is unfeathered.
5. The contour and body feathers are lightly edged with white.
6. Two races of bald eagles occur in North America. The northern race is larger and darker than the southern race.
7. These birds are frequently but not always found near open water or rivers.
8. The bald eagle feeds mainly on fish and waterfowl, often pirating prey from smaller raptors rather than hunting for itself.

5 1/2"–6"

Eye
16mm
straw yellow

32"–40"

23"+

19"+

Scholz '92

Bald Eagle
Haliaeetus leucocephalus

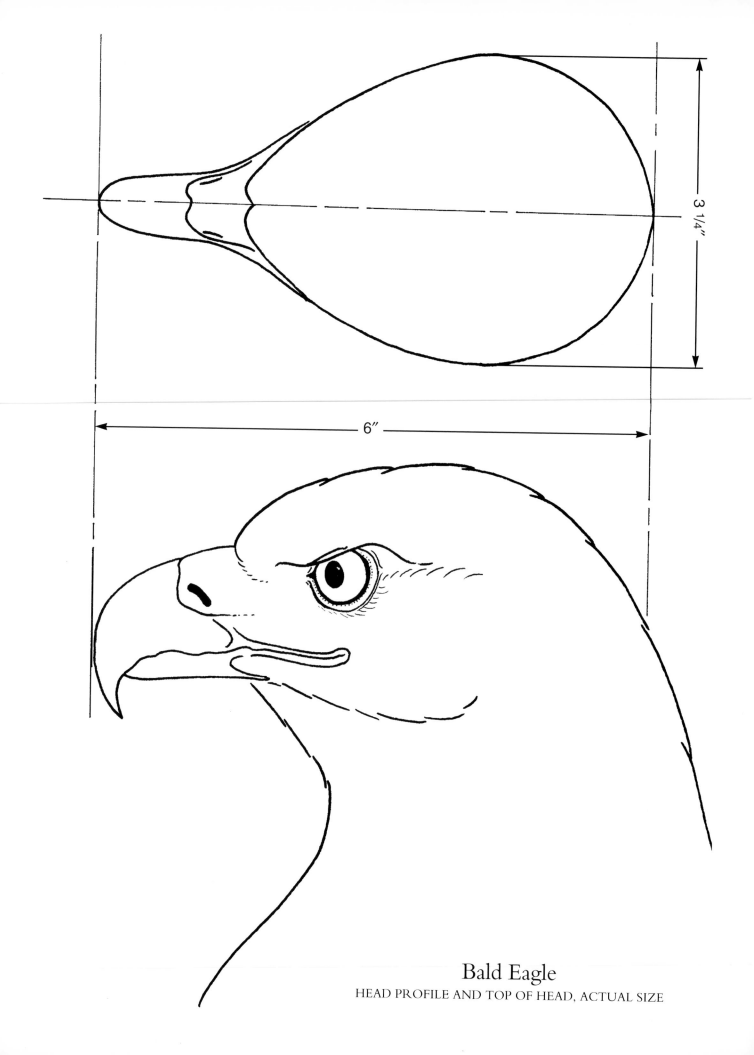

3 1/4"

6"

Bald Eagle

HEAD PROFILE AND TOP OF HEAD, ACTUAL SIZE

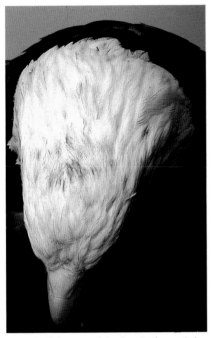

Detail of the top of the head of an adult bald eagle.

Detail of the interior of an adult bald eagle's mouth.

The protective translucent membrane that shields the eye from dust and airborne particles is known as the nictitating membrane.

Head profile showing the extremely large mouth opening. Note how the tongue extends out beyond the lower mandible.

The flexibility of the corners of the mouth allows an extremely wide gape.

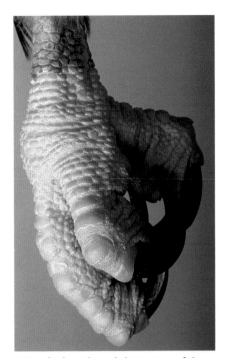

Note the heavily scaled structure of this clenched foot. It appears as though the largest and roundest of the scales are located directly above the joint of each toe.

The interesting transition from feathers to fleshy cere. Also note the shape and structure of the eyelid and fleshy lobe protruding beyond the brow.

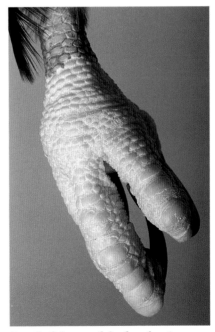

Detail of the top of the foot showing rows and rows of small, flexible scales.

This three-quarter front view shows the flatness of the sides of the head and the pronounced lip extending to directly below the eye.

The color shades of the underwing coverts vary from gray-blue to warm brown.

The shapes and patterns of feathers and feather groups are more easily distinguished on the body of an eagle in subadult plumage.

A majestic, partially spread-winged subadult. Notice the heavily notched primaries visible on both wings.

This is a four-year-old bald eagle. With the next molt the bird will achieve the typical pure white head and solid reddish brown body of an adult bird.

The long neck and large, bulbous bill of this young bald eagle are typical of the sea eagle family to which it belongs.

A subadult bald eagle preens itself. This beautiful photo of the back area shows the position and relationships of all the major feather groups.

This front view shows the narrow bill and binocular con-figuration of the eyes.

Close-up of the scapulars, tertials, and major flight feathers of a subadult bald eagle.

The alert pose and flared wings of a young eagle about to launch itself off its perch.

Head profile of an adult American bald eagle.

*Opposite page: A nice side view of an
adult bald eagle.*

Opposite page and above: Various head and posture studies of an American bald eagle.

Golden Eagle
Aquila chrysaetos

"BIRD OF JOVE" IS ONE OF THE MANY ALIASES GIVEN to the king of birds, revered in ancient Rome as the legendary messenger of the god Jove (Jupiter) and thought to have thunderbolts in its talons as it sped across the heavens. A world away, ancient Native American civilizations worshiped a deity known as the thunderbird, a link between mortals and the Great Spirit. It is interesting that two distinct civilizations so isolated from each other could share such similar feelings toward one animal. Such is the power of the great golden eagle.

"The farther from humans the better." If golden eagles could speak, I'm sure that's what they would say. Birds of remote mountainous regions rising above the vast open spaces of the West, in America golden eagles symbolize true wilderness. Patrolling valleys and mountains, golden eagles nest on cliffs, building gigantic stick nests that offer a solid platform on which to raise their young.

Dry ornithological facts will reveal that *Aquila chrysaetos* is a large brown raptor between 30 and 38 inches long, found worldwide in remote mountainous regions of the northern hemisphere, represented by seven races, and feeding on a variety of mammals up to the size of small deer. But to accurately put forth a description, one must go beyond the mere facts. In Arthur Cleveland Bent's *Life Histories of North American Birds* the golden eagle is best summarized in one paragraph: "This magnificent eagle has long been named the king of birds, and it well deserves the title. It is majestic in flight, regal in appearance, dignified in manner, and crowned with golden hackles about its royal head. When falconry flourished in Europe the golden eagle was flown only by the kings."

The power of the golden eagle's crushing feet is truly amazing. The long, thick talons of the rear and inside toes are the size of grizzly bear claws and can penetrate up to three inches into a victim.

Relying on acute eyesight to locate prey, the golden eagle will soar for hours surveying its territory in search of the prairie dogs and ground squirrels that make up the bulk of its diet. Once a target is sighted, the golden eagle will bank sharply from its lofty vantage point and rifle in fast and low, zipping around small hills that offer concealment, to deftly pick off its unsuspecting quarry.

With so many outstanding qualities found in one bird, it comes as no surprise that the golden eagle is considered by many to be the most highly evolved of all birds of prey. I can find little reason to dispute that belief.

SPECIES PROFILE

1. The body is extremely large (from 30 to 38 inches long) and totally brown.
2. The sexes differ slightly in size; females are larger and heavier.
3. The bill is dark blue at the tip, gradually shading to light bluish gray.
4. The cere and toes are pale yellow.
5. The neck is feathered with golden-edged contour feathers down to the nape area on the back and to the chest in front.
6. The eyes are deep brown set under a heavy brow ridge. Eye color does not change as the eagle matures.
7. The legs are densely feathered down to the top of the toes.
8. The tail is mottled brown in adult plumage and rounded at the end when folded.
9. The inside and rear talons are disproportionately large and daggerlike, sometimes exceeding 3 inches in length.

5 ½"

*Eye
18mm
dark brown*

32"-39"

25"-27"

19"-20"

Golden Eagle
Aquila chrysaetos

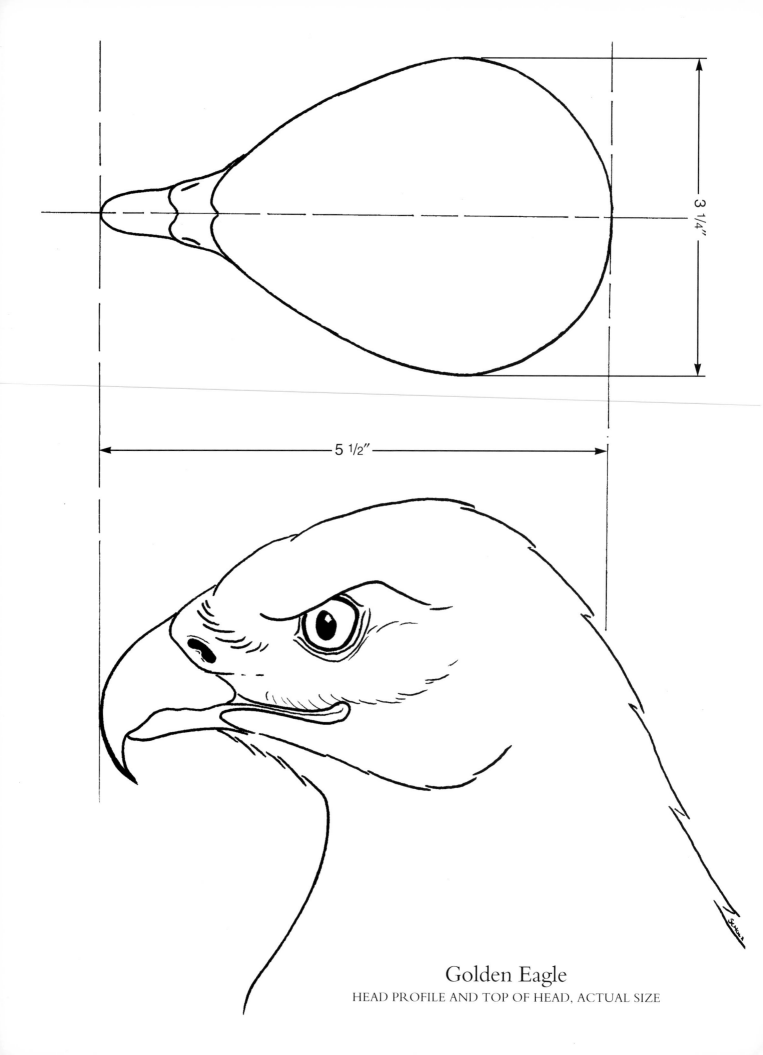

3 1/4"

5 1/2"

Golden Eagle
HEAD PROFILE AND TOP OF HEAD, ACTUAL SIZE

The profile of this golden eagle shows its head structure is drastically different from that of the bald eagle.

A three-quarter front close-up of bill and nostril detail.

The nictitating membrane covering the eye seems to have a bluish cast.

The golden yellow nape feathers on the back of the head are what give this extraordinary bird its name.

Back view of the head showing the directional flow of the spear-shaped feathers.

Back view of an adult golden eagle looking over its shoulder.

The bright white underfeathers show through and strongly contrast with the deep brown contour feathers.

The dry scale of the cere and bill can clearly be seen in this photo, as can the growth marks on the upper mandible.

A close-up of the lore area in front of the eye.

Feather shape changes drastically, becoming more scalloped where the wing inserts into the shoulder feathers.

The enormous, heavily scaled feet of an adult golden eagle. Notice how far down the tarsus feathers extend.

Extreme close-up of the secondary coverts showing the fine details of the feather structure.

The right foot reveals the incredible size and killing ability of the hallux, or rear toe.

The photo sequence on the next four pages is a study
of the attitudes and postures of an adult golden eagle from
various angles.

OSPREY
Pandion haliáetus

OSPREY
(IMMATURE)
STREAKED CROWN, LIGHT
FEATHER TIPS, DARKER
EYE

REED A. PRESCOTT III

Osprey
Pandion haliaetus

IN TERMS OF PHYSICAL DESIGN THE OSPREY IS A superbly adapted raptor ideally suited to locate, pursue, and catch its slippery prey. Since the osprey is neither an eagle nor a hawk, it has the distinction of being the sole representative of its own genus. The large "fish eagle" is easy to identify in flight due to its large white body, narrow wings, and high-arched-wing flight characteristic. Ospreys are often seen flying over or near open bodies of water on a constant lookout for surface-swimming fish. Once a fish is sighted, the osprey will hover as if deciding its plan of attack, then tuck its long wings and plummet straight down, legs fully extended, charging into the water with a huge splash, often emerging with a silvery squirming fish in its talons.

Ospreys are found on every continent except Antarctica (they are also absent from New Zealand). They construct large, visible nests by piling a jumble of sticks in the crotch of a tall tree, usually overlooking a body of water. Quite vocal, the osprey is often heard before it is seen returning to the nest with its most recent catch.

The most unique part of an osprey's anatomy has to be its feet. A specially designed toe configuration and an abundance of spiny projections covering the pads, known as spicules, aid in assuring a non-slip grip. Ospreys have the unique ability to swivel the outside toe either to the front or rear of the foot depending on the grip necessary to hold on to their evasive quarry.

Almost completely wiped out in America due to the cumulative effects of DDT and other chlorinated hydrocarbons, ospreys are once again gracing the skies over shimmering waters, slowly recovering from yet another in a long list of human environmental blunders. With the osprey once again breeding and sailing the skies over its long-abandoned range, we can breathe a sigh of relief . . . at least for now.

SPECIES PROFILE

1. The osprey is a large-sized bird, ranging from 21 to 24½ inches; females are larger than males.
2. Its belly, breast, and head are white.
3. The bill is all black, the legs gray-blue.
4. Adult ospreys have bright yellow eyes and a distinct brown eye stripe.
5. Their large, powerful feet are heavily scaled with sharp spikes called spicules.
6. The osprey is the only diurnal raptor with completely round talons. The talons have an extremely curved shape and are quite long.
7. The long, pointed wings afford extreme heavy lift capabilities.
8. Ospreys fly with their wings highly arched.
9. They nest and live close to open water, both fresh and salt.
10. They feed only on fish and marine animals.

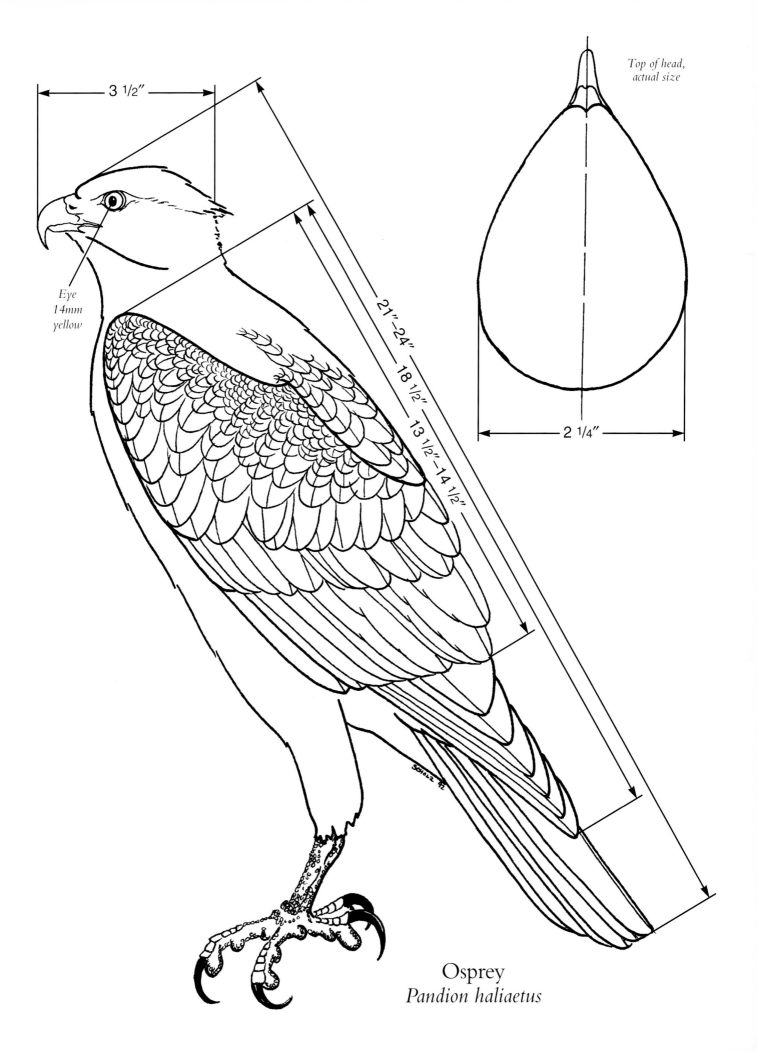

3 1/2"

Eye
14mm
yellow

21"–24"

18 1/2"

13 1/2"–14 1/2"

Top of head,
actual size

2 1/4"

Scholz '92

Osprey
Pandion haliaetus

MICHAEL L. SMITH

The noble lord of the waterways. Adult ospreys usually choose perches that afford a broad, unobstructed view of open water, making them one of the most conspicuous of large North American raptors.

MICHAEL L. SMITH

Ever on the lookout for a potential meal, the osprey misses little with its watchful gaze. Note the extreme length of the wing tips as they pass over the tail.

When the osprey is alarmed, its long crest feathers stand erect, framing the intense face and adding to the bird's unique look.

One of the more vocal birds of prey, the osprey is often heard before it is seen.

MICHAEL L. SMITH

ERNIE SIMMONS

Note the eye-to-bill relationship and strong arch of the nostril openings.

ERNIE SIMMONS

Feet, legs, undertail coverts, and lower tail surfaces are clearly laid out in this photo. An osprey's tail when spread has a rounded end.

ERNIE SIMMONS

The flow of feathers around the eye and on the side of the head is accentuated by the distinct dark brown eye stripe.

The corners of the mouth cavity stretch and form two vertical walls, allowing the mouth to open wide. Note the shape of the tongue and how it relates to the lower mandible. This unfortunate bird is an immature that was brought into the nature center already dead.

The roof of the mouth of the inside upper mandible shows the unique structure found on most diurnal birds of prey.

Left: This alert osprey has its crest feathers erect. Note how the dark brown eye stripe flows down and onto the back.

The osprey's feet and talons are exceptionally well suited for catching fish and other aquatic foods. Note the extremely heavy scaling on the leg or tarsus.

ERNIE SIMMONS

ERNIE SIMMONS

An osprey can position its toes two different ways. The perching configuration in the foreground is known as a zygodactyl arrangement; the background foot held with three toes forward and rear toe back displays an anisodactyl arrangement.

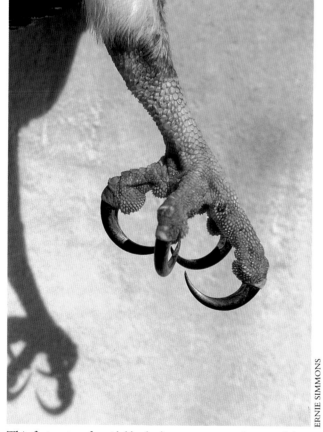

ERNIE SIMMONS

This foot casts a formidable shadow, sure to terrorize any fish.

ERNIE SIMMONS

The osprey's outer toe is able to swivel both forward and back.

A large jumble of sticks atop a pole or tree near open water is a sure sign of nesting ospreys. This adult osprey is about to land on its nest. Note the distinct crook of the wing and length of the legs.

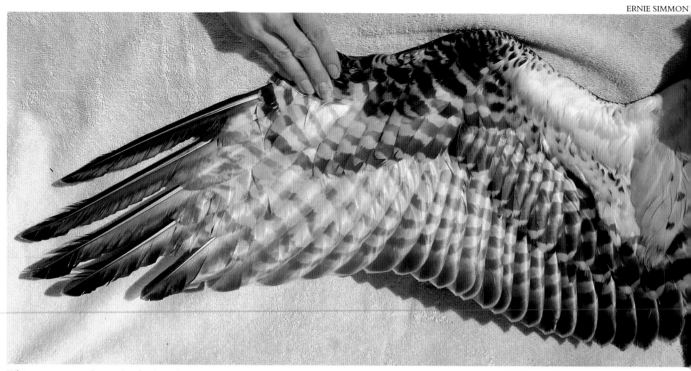

This open wing shows the feather shape, size, and plumage patterns of an adult's underwing feathers. Note the heavily notched outer primaries and graceful sweep of the under-secondary coverts.

A close-up of the underside of this osprey's wing shows the shape and location of the axillary feathers.

The upper surface of a young osprey's outstretched wing. Young ospreys have a pronounced white tip on all the contour feathers.

ERNIE SIMMONS

Note the long and extremely well-developed primary covert feathers. An adult osprey can haul fish weighing up to four pounds up and out of the water.

ERNIE SIMMONS

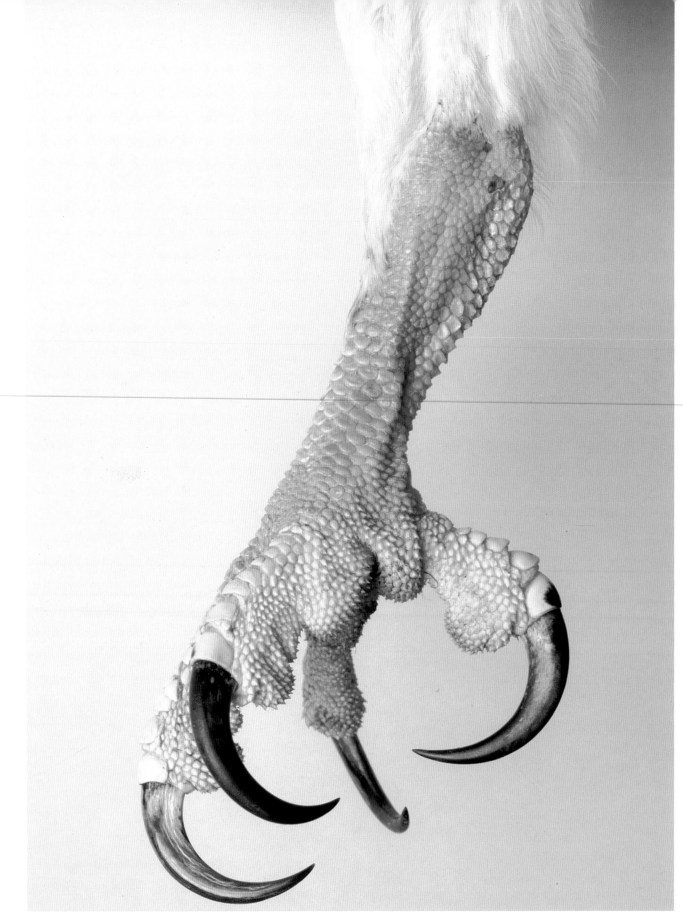

The superbly adapted feet of the osprey have extremely sharp and strongly curved talons. The fleshy pads under the toes have special little spikes that aid in holding on to slippery fish. Also note the thickness of the toes, the well-developed tarsus area, and the fine, flexible scale patterns.

The long, high-arching wing design allows the osprey to carry much heavier weight loads in relation to body size than any other bird of prey. Note the heavy notching on the first four primaries.

The upper surface of the wing of a young osprey shows the long, slender primaries and tightly compacted secondaries and secondary coverts. The wing feathers are longer, thinner, and more numerous on an osprey than on other large raptors.

Techniques for the Artist and Carver

REGARDLESS OF AN ARTIST'S ABILITIES, HE OR SHE IS only as good as the reference materials available. Thus far in this book we have dealt with a select group of North American raptors, illustrating the physical characteristics unique to each species. (Keep in mind, of course, that among these featured birds size, shape, and coloration can vary tremendously.)

Creating something of beauty that can touch and inspire the viewer is the ultimate vision of any artist. To see beyond the obvious, to interpret images so that they instill perspective and enrichment in everyday life, is to fulfill that vision. In striving to achieve these rather ambitious goals, one must have a solid working knowledge of the chosen medium, whether in painting or sculpting. Painters must learn to mix colors and apply them with a brush or palette knife, while a sculptor must learn to remove excess materials while refining the block to the desired shape. To achieve any artistic goal, basic techniques must first be mastered, because these provide the foundation on which to build.

Contemporary wooden bird sculpture is unique to the world of art. To produce a truly spectacular piece of work, the bird sculptor must master many different skills. A thorough knowledge of ornithology and avian anatomy is absolutely essential. One must have the skills of a sculptor and be able to draw. Understanding color and its application is necessary to achieve an illusion of depth and softness on an otherwise hard, resilient surface. Woodworking skills are also important, as is an understanding of the inherent properties of certain woods. Putting it all together takes the skill of an engineer, and an aptitude for metal working certainly is helpful as many accessories, such as feet, are commonly made of steel or brass. In short, to become a world-class bird sculptor one must be a truly multifaceted artist and craftsman.

Often I'm asked which of the two disciplines, carving or painting, I enjoy most. In the overall process, few things can match the excitement I feel when a rough block of wood slowly takes shape as a recognizable form, emulating the smooth, seductive curves of a living bird's body, ultimately taking on a life of its own. But the application of color, visually converting a hard surface into something that can fool the eye of the viewer, putting the final brush strokes on a feather group and having it suddenly come alive—this for me is where the true magic of the art form is found.

When it comes to carving and painting a wooden bird it is usually the carver-artist's ability (or lack thereof) to paint that most affects the final appearance. Often a beautifully carved work can be ruined by an inferior paint job; on the other hand, a rather plain, uninteresting carving can be brought to life by virtue of an outstanding painting technique. During the seminars I've taught, it is usually the painting that seems to create the most anxiety and frustration for the bird carving student. Painting is an area in which most students of the art form feel they can stand improvement. In the following section I will attempt to uncover some of the mysteries of painting as I share various techniques I employ to achieve softness, subtlety, and variety in an effort to express the essence of the living bird.

HEAD FLOW

BACK FLOW

BREAST FLOW

WING FLOW

Convergent feather pattern flow on the head, breast, back, and wing coverts of a diurnal raptor. Understanding the interrelationships of the various feather tracts is essential in order to correctly map out directional feather patterns on body areas other than the major flight feathers.

SCHOLZ '92

Ferruginous Hawk
HEAD PROFILE, ACTUAL SIZE

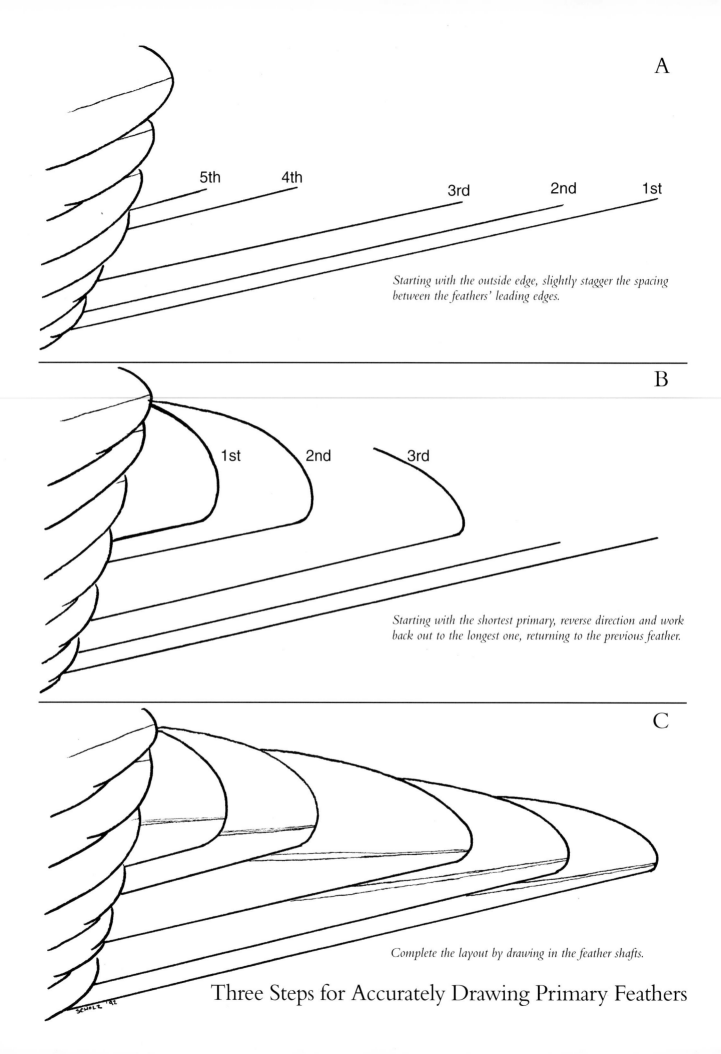

A

5th 4th 3rd 2nd 1st

Starting with the outside edge, slightly stagger the spacing between the feathers' leading edges.

B

1st 2nd 3rd

Starting with the shortest primary, reverse direction and work back out to the longest one, returning to the previous feather.

C

Complete the layout by drawing in the feather shafts.

Three Steps for Accurately Drawing Primary Feathers

Painting the American Kestrel

PERHAPS NO OTHER BIRD OF PREY HAS BEEN SO OFTEN chosen as a subject for the carver-artist's first attempt at raptor carving than the male American kestrel. Its combination of small size, beautiful coloration, and familiarity all add up to its being a favorite among bird carvers. It is large enough to give one a sense of satisfaction upon completion, yet not so large as to overwhelm the beginner.

Every facet of painting technique is employed to paint a kestrel. Distinct patterning and subtle blending are just two of the many characteristics that demand total focus and concentration.

Prior to starting, I would like to stress several points.

Number one: when it comes to paint brushes, buy only the best! This is one area where attempting to skimp and save a buck will bring you frustration and headaches. A top-quality brush will benefit you in many ways: it will hold more paint, afford much more control, and last much longer than a cheap brand.

Number two: be patient! As an artist your ultimate goal is to achieve an illusion of softness on your carving. This can only be done if the paint is applied in thin, translucent wash coats, not in thick, opaque layers. Many of the world's top carver-artists do a lot of painting with very little paint. Learning to let the paint work for you instead of against you can only be achieved with lots of practice!

Number three: develop a painting strategy. Study the plumage of the subject you want to portray and decide how best to achieve the desired effect. Remember to always paint from light to dark.

Materials needed to paint a wooden bird have changed very little over the years. What has changed is the chemical makeup of the paints (i.e., acrylics versus oils) and the development and usage of the airbrush. Although I have a hundred or so brushes in my studio, I tend to use just three or four specific sizes for all of my painting. My favorite brush is the Raphael 8408 series, and the sizes I use are the #1, #4, and #6. With these three sizes I can paint anything ranging from a hair-thin line up to large overlay wash coats. I paint with acrylics — I've found that, for me, they render a softer, subtler look and have the added advantage of drying quickly. Often I use a hot-air blow-dryer to speed the drying of wash coats, thus cutting down on the monotony one often encounters when laying in wash after wash.

Paint manufacturers all tout the wonderful virtues of their respective paints, but after trying out most of the top brands I haven't found any appreciable differences among them, with one major exception. Among the earth tones — raw umber, burnt umber, raw sienna, and burnt sienna — distinct color variations do exist, so be aware of this fact and always test the color on a scrap piece of material prior to final application. It is very helpful to make a paint board before you begin painting; 1/8- to 1/4-inch tempered Masonite works well. Apply four to five coats of white gesso primer to ensure total coverage of the 8-by-10-inch panel.

Write down your color mixes as you proceed so you have a record for future reference. Above all, don't be afraid to experiment and explore new ideas. Mistakes are inevitable, so use them as learning experiences rather than as points of frustration.

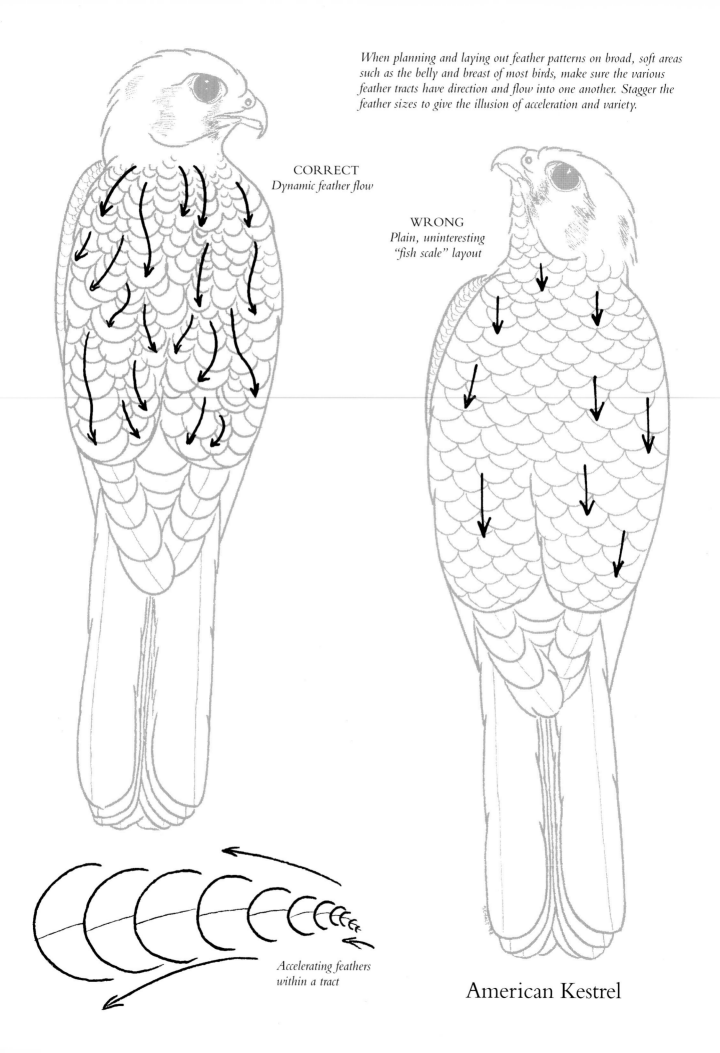

When planning and laying out feather patterns on broad, soft areas such as the belly and breast of most birds, make sure the various feather tracts have direction and flow into one another. Stagger the feather sizes to give the illusion of acceleration and variety.

CORRECT
Dynamic feather flow

WRONG
Plain, uninteresting "fish scale" layout

Accelerating feathers within a tract

American Kestrel

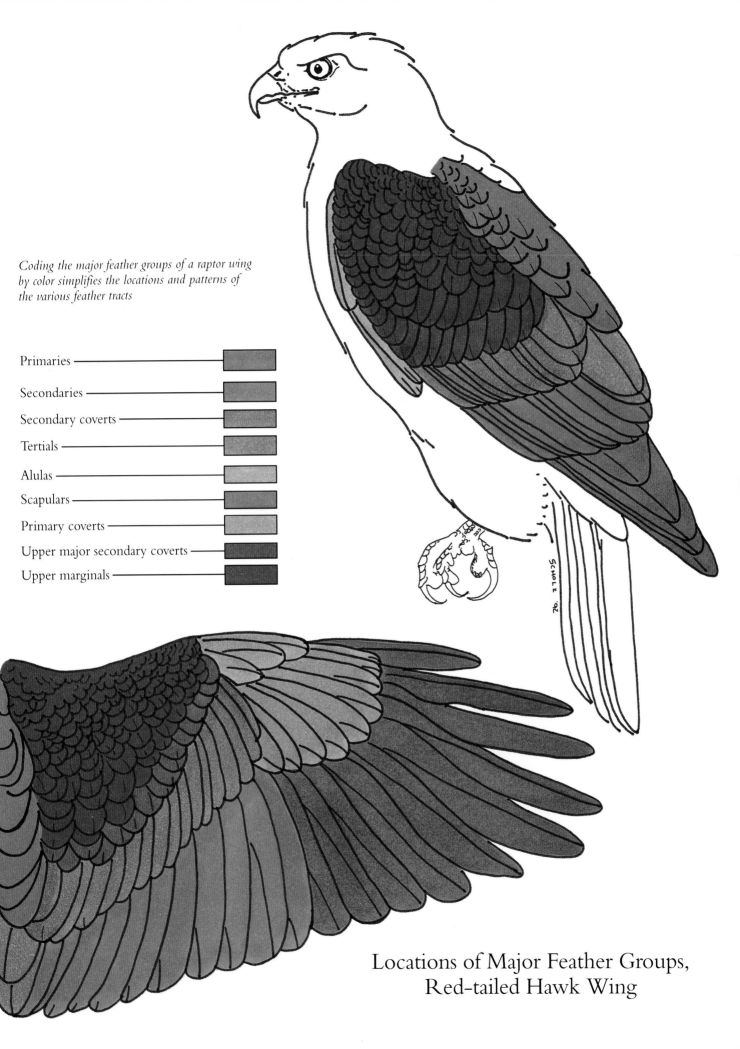

Coding the major feather groups of a raptor wing
by color simplifies the locations and patterns of
the various feather tracts

Primaries

Secondaries

Secondary coverts

Tertials

Alulas

Scapulars

Primary coverts

Upper major secondary coverts

Upper marginals

Locations of Major Feather Groups,
Red-tailed Hawk Wing

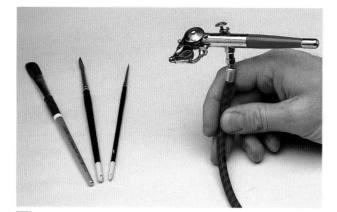

1 The basic tools used in addition to paints are as follows left to right: Simmons half-inch oval wash brush, #6 Raphael 8408, #1 sable brush, and a Pasche A-B turbo airbrush with compressor.

2 Brush: half-inch oval wash (Simmons or Liquitex). After thoroughly brushing out and cleaning the surface of the carving, apply two coats of wood sealer. Then prime the bird with three to four thin wash coats of Liquitex gesso thinned with water and a couple drops of flow medium.

3 Strive to achieve a uniform covering of the entire surface. On burned areas, some darker coloring will still show through; this is a desirable effect as it will add to the shading of the feathers.

4 All of the major feather groups are clearly defined and ready for the application of color.

5 *Brush: Pasche A-B turbo airbrush with 28 pounds of pressure. Mix 40% burnt umber and 60% ultramarine blue to get a warm bluish gray, then lighten this mixture with a bit of gesso to get a medium gray. Airbrush this gray mixture into all the valleys to amplify the depths of the belly and chest areas. Lightly outline each feather throughout the underside and the undertail coverts.*

6 *Brush: #6 Raphael. Warm up the high areas with a thin wash of cadmium red light.*

7 *Study a skin of the real bird and take time to develop a painting strategy. Look for the subtleties in the plumage and plan your paint applications accordingly.*

8 *Brush: half-inch oval wash. Aside from white, the lightest colors are found on the tail and back areas. For these areas mix 80% burnt sienna with 20% burnt umber, and layer on up to eight thin wash coats until the desired shade is achieved. Also paint the top of the head with this same mixture.*

9   *Brush: #6 Raphael. Starting from the tail and working forward allows you to correctly overlap feathers quite easily, and gives you a chance to warm up before tackling more prominent areas. Block in the subterminal band of the tail with a mix of 50% burnt umber, 40% ultramarine blue, 10% carbon black, and a few drops of flow medium. Paint the primaries with the same paint mixture.*

10   *Continue to blend the washes and shade certain areas to increase the color intensity.*

11   *Hopscotch around and outline certain feathers with additional washes of the burnt sienna and burnt umber mixture to accentuate individual feathers and feather tracts.*

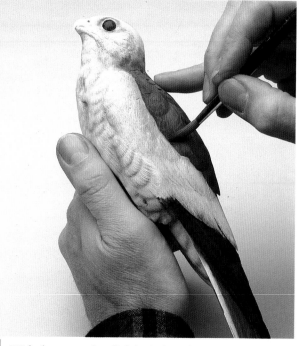

12   *With the same color slightly darken the outer sides of the back. This accentuates the curvature of the side area and helps highlight the junction of the two converging feather groups.*

13 *To achieve some visual diversity on an otherwise plainly colored group of feathers such as these primaries, pick out and darken certain feathers so they stand out.*

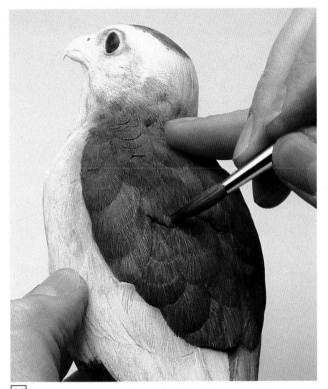

14 *Finalize the back color and make adjustments if necessary.*

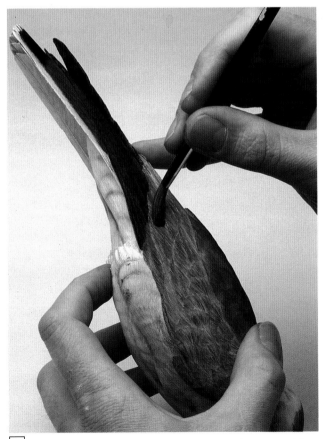

15 *With a mix of 80% Payne's gray, 20% ultramarine blue, and a drop of flow medium, wash the secondaries and the entire remaining wing area.*

16 *Repeat the same techniques used on the back area to high-light certain feathers and feather groups.*

17 *Continue the application of wash coats until the desired intensity is achieved. Remember to avoid uniformity in color—paint some feathers darker than others.*

18 *Brush: #1 Raphael. After studying your references, paint the inner edges of the primaries with quick, distinct brush strokes to highlight the burn lines. Begin with 70% warm white and 30% raw umber and then, with successive layers, go to straight warm white on the extreme outer edges.*

19 *Follow the same procedure and finish the tip of the tail.*

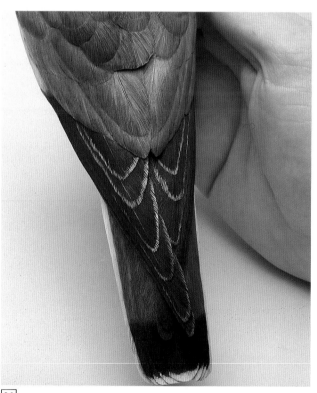

20 *The completed upper tail and crossed primaries. The base color has also been completed, and the upper wing surfaces and entire back area are now ready for the dark barring and related detailing.*

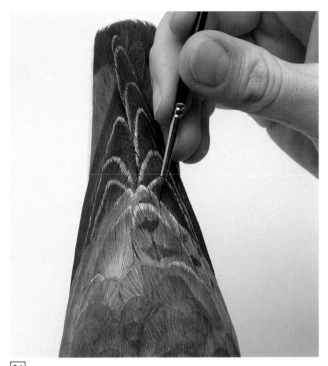

21 *Highlight the outer edges of the tertials and secondaries using the same procedures covered in step 18. Block in the black barring of the tertials and secondaries with light wash coats of 50% ultramarine blue and 50% burnt umber.*

22 *Lightly dampen the feather surface prior to painting on the dark patterns. This allows for a more subtle edge between the dark paint and the lighter blue feather surface.*

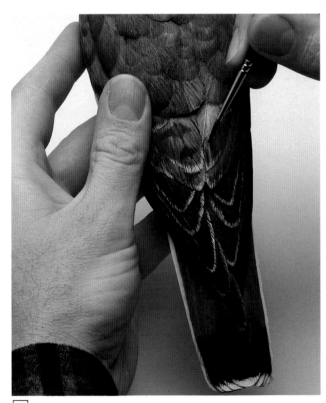

23 *Still using the #1 brush, apply feather highlights and accents such as feather splits and subtle shading.*

24 *Continue to work your way up the wing, adding and deepening existing dark barring and occasionally going over lighter edges of feathers to make them stand out.*

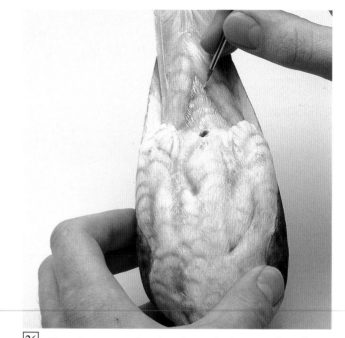

26 *Once the upper tail, primaries, and wing areas have been completed, it's time to work on the underside of the tail and undertail coverts. Drag pure white gesso mixed with a small amount of flow medium back over the darker valleys to give the illusion of hairlike, soft-edged feathers.*

25 *Spend time adjusting the color intensities of both the base color and the dark bars and spots. The distinct black spots should be painted in so they accentuate the feather flow of the wing and shoulder area.*

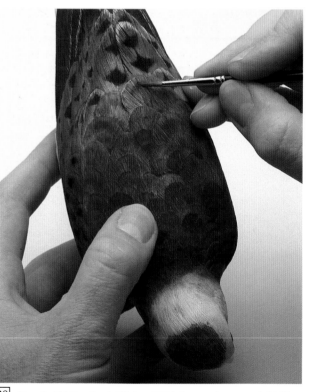

27 *Brush: #6 Raphael. Mix 50% ultramarine blue, 40% burnt umber, and 10% carbon black. Lay out and slowly paint in the black patterns of the tail undersides. Remember to slightly dampen the surface first.*

28 *Brush: #1 Raphael. Using 70% burnt sienna and 30% warm white, lightly edge the scapular feathers all the way up to the back of the head.*

29 Brush: #6 Raphael. Paint in the dark barring on the scapulars and shoulder areas. Frequently check your references to ensure accuracy, since not every feather has the dark markings.

30 The barring decreases in size as the feathers get smaller. Take advantage of this feature to accentuate feather flow.

31 Spend time highlighting critical feather junctions. Emphasize feather overlap by painting in splits and breaks with a darker value, then dragging the lighter value of the top feather color onto the lower group.

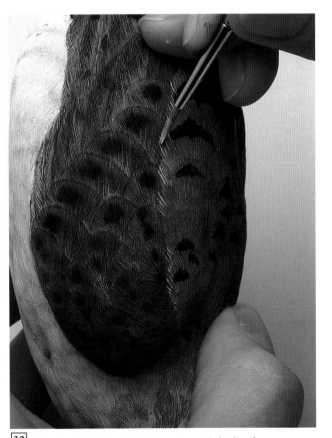

32 Brush: #1 Raphael. Work up toward the head.

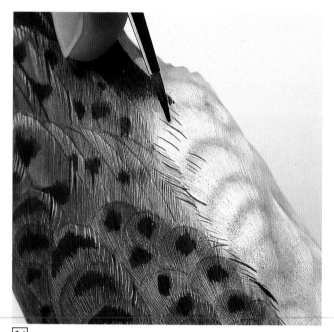

33 *Make final adjustments to individual feathers.*

34 *To really show off the long, soft-edged flank feathers, first paint in the splits with a mixture of 70% Payne's gray and 30% burnt umber.*

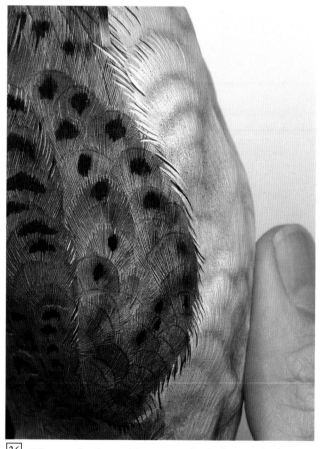

35 *Then drag straight gesso mixed with a small amount of flow medium back over the wings following the carved texture.*

36 *The completed transition zones of soft, flowing feathers over hard-edged, darker feathers.*

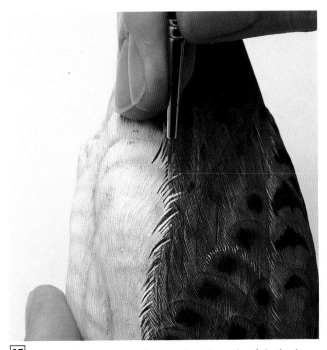

37 *Repeat the same procedure on the other side of the bird.*

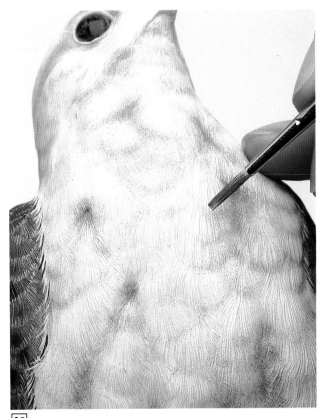

38 *A tremendous amount of care must be taken when painting in the soft-flowing feathers of the belly and chest areas. Be prepared to spend lots of time brushstroking the individual hairlike feather edges.*

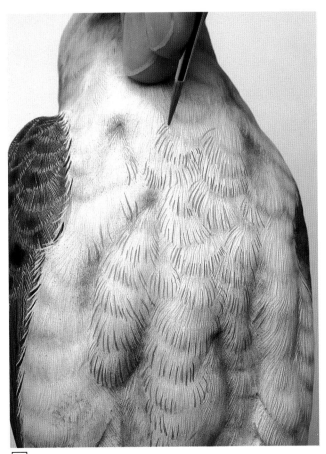

39 *With a warm gray mixture of 30% ultramarine blue, 30% burnt umber, and 30% gesso, paint in the splits and separations of the feathers.*

40 *Drag pure white gesso back over the darker underfeathers.*

41 *After all the finicky brushwork, it's satisfying to lay on nice subtle washes of color to homogenize the feather group. Switching to a half-inch oval wash brush, wash a mix of 70% burnt sienna and 30% yellow ochre onto the whole upper chest area.*

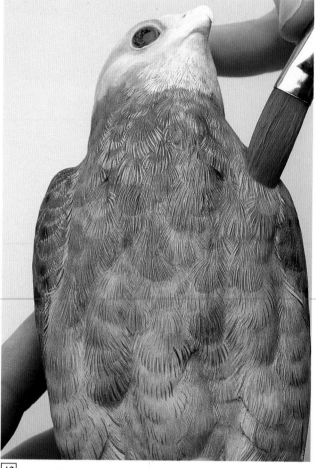

42 *Build the intensity of the area with successive wash coats of the same mixture. Be extremely careful not to apply the colors too thickly or opaquely, as you will cover up all of your hard work underneath.*

43 *Brush: #1 Raphael. With unbleached titanium and a small amount of flow medium, highlight the edges of the cape and shoulder feathers.*

44 *Carry this edging onto the upper breast area for certain feathers.*

45 *Brush: #6 Raphael. Using the same techniques and color described earlier, paint in the black teardrop marking along the flanks and leading up onto the chest.*

46 *With 40% ultramarine blue, 40% burnt umber, and 20% carbon black, paint in the distinctive malar striping along the cheeks and back of the head, following your reference photos and/or live specimen.*

47 *Before painting the bill, paint the cere and eye rings with yellow ochre and highlight with thin washes of burnt sienna around the nostril area. Then paint the entire bill (top and bottom mandibles) with 60% Payne's gray and 40% warm white. Keep this surface damp and begin building up the darkness of the bill tip with straight Payne's gray. This is an area where the airbrush can be quite useful to achieve a subtle color transition between light and dark. Once the bill has been painted, overlay the blue areas with a mixture of matte medium and water, polyurethane, or any type of good flat varnish.*

48 *Brush: #6 Raphael. Wash in and darken the blue areas around the top of the head with 70% Payne's gray and 30% ultramarine blue, using lots of water to aid in blending the areas together.*

49 *Brush: #1 Raphael. With a mix of 40% yellow ochre and 60% raw umber, carefully paint in the line separating the upper and lower mandibles, extending it out along the lips to directly below the eye.*

50 *Along the cheek draw straight gesso from the white areas onto the black stripes.*

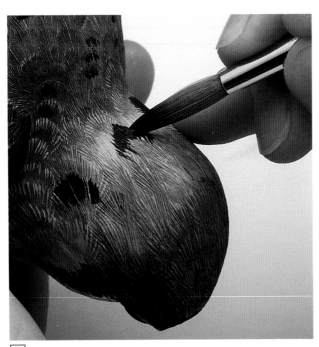

51 *Continue work on the back of the head by deepening the black spots and dragging color from the lighter feathers onto the black.*

52 *The chin area is composed of very soft, fluffy white feathers. Paint them with warm white and flow medium, gently flicking the edges to accentuate the hairlike quality of this feather group.*

53 *Detail around the eye ring with burnt sienna, highlighting the minute folds and creases around the eye and fleshy lore area.*

54 *Go back and tighten up areas that you may have overlooked, such as these tail edges and feather tips.*

55 *With straight carbon black, drag the hairlike feathers of the rear edge of the facial stripes onto the lighter area.*

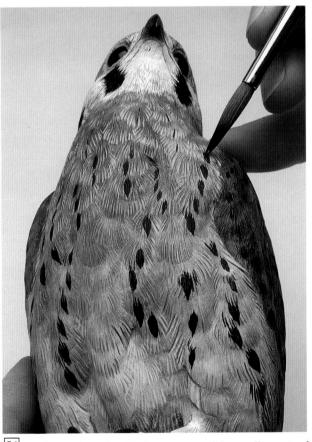

56 *Dab straight carbon black onto some of the smaller spots of the upper breast area. Vary the darkness of the spots to avoid monotony.*

58 Look the whole head over and make final color adjustments to certain areas. Study your references!

57 The nostril baffle is a straight pin inserted into the nostril opening. Still using the #1 brush, dab a bit of yellow oxide on the top to accentuate it.

59 A white Styrofoam plate makes a great palette: when you've run out of room with your mixes, just dispose of it and start fresh.

60 This close-up profile of the completed head shows what a little careful brushwork can do to enhance the soft, feathery look.

61 A three-quarter front view. Notice the bill details, malar strips, and white chin area.

62 Careful attention must be paid to areas such as this now completed back.

63 Full view of the finished back, primaries, and tail.

64 Left side, full view. (Note the unfinished feet: the toes are carved of tupelo and the legs are made of 1/16-inch copper wire and two-part plumber's epoxy putty. The talons are made of Super Sculpey modeling compound.)

65　*A three-quarter back view of the painted American kestrel.*

66　*The kestrel is now totally finished except for the feet. The rocks are made of 2-inch rigid building insulation glued up and then bandsawed to shape. The rock exterior is Durham rock-hard water putty troweled on and textured with a stiff-bristle brush. The rocks are painted with gesso primer, and then many light, watery wash coats of 50% ultramarine blue and 50% burnt umber are allowed to run down and flow into all of the nooks and crevices of the rough rock surface. Cracks and splits are then highlighted with a dark grayish black mixture applied with a #6 Raphael sable brush. The base is oiled black walnut cut free-form to match the shape of the bottom rock; then the top edge is rounded over with a hand-held router.*

Sculpting a Raptor Head

USING A FEW BASIC GEOMETRIC PRINCIPLES, YOU CAN achieve balance and proportion with little effort while sculpting a raptor head. It is important to give this part of the carving careful attention. No matter what your skill at carving, if the head is not symmetrical and the eyes are not set correctly, the bird will lack the all-important spark of life so essential to a bird of prey. When sculpting my hawks, eagles, and falcons, I am constantly striving to capture the essence of the species.

Subtle differences in head shape and size exist among the species. Among the falcons, for example, the female, being the larger and heavier of the pair, has a proportionately bigger and rounder head than the male.

The following sequence of photos illustrates the simple rules I follow when sculpting a diurnal raptor's head. These techniques can be applied to any hawk or eagle with success as long as the center lines are firmly established and maintained. These are the basic guidelines and of course should be adapted to suit the species you're carving.

1 With lots of extra wood to spare, establish the top center line indicating the direction the hawk will be looking.

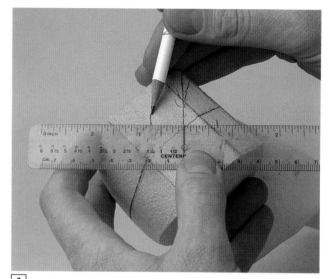

2 The width of the head is measured out and two parallel lines are drawn in the direction of the top center line, establishing the outer dimension of the head and neck.

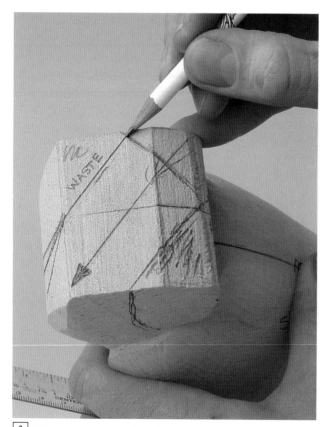

3 The waste wood is then eliminated.

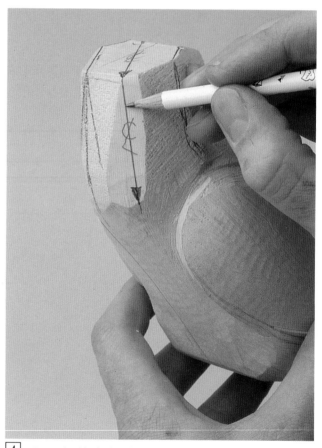

4 Once the blocked-in head shape is achieved, locate and sketch the front center line. It is important to remember that the top and front center lines are essential in maintaining symmetry throughout the sculpting process and if they are sanded out they should be redrawn immediately.

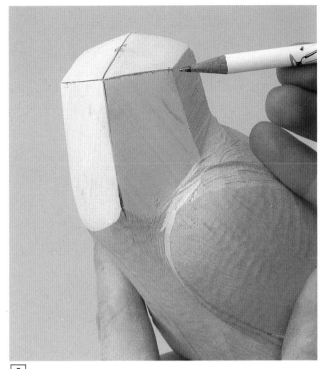

5 The front facets are shaped to even off the front section of the head and sanded smooth. Now, a symmetrical, geometric shape has been achieved, allowing for a much easier layout of final head dimension.

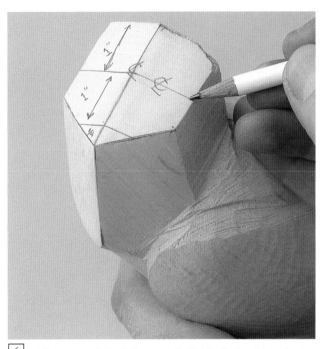

6 Allow ¼ inch for bill material, divide the head lengthwise, and draw in a crosshatch line that establishes the exact top of the head. This will be important when it comes time to lay out and drill the eye holes.

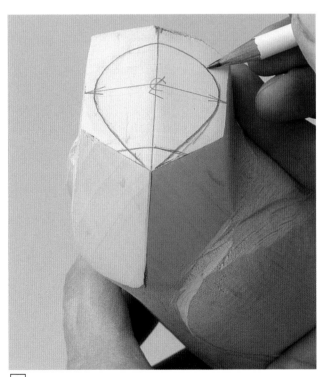

7 Using measurements taken from a live bird, draw a pattern of the top of the head and transfer it to the block, establishing the exact dimensions of the head.

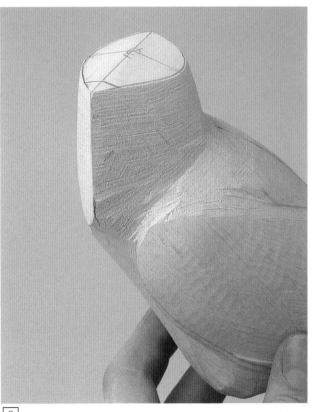

8 The excess wood has been carved away leaving a well-shaped head ready for additional refinements.

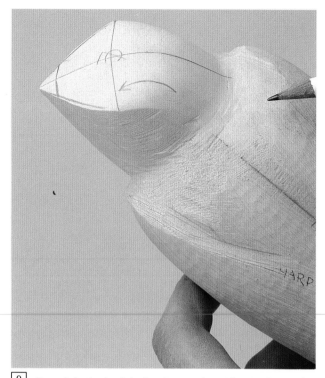

9 *Round the back of the head up to the mid-point line and sand smooth.*

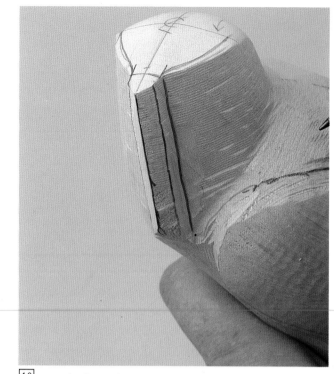

10 *On the front of the head, carefully lay out and block in the bill. The front sides of the head will need to be tapered to the vertical lines.*

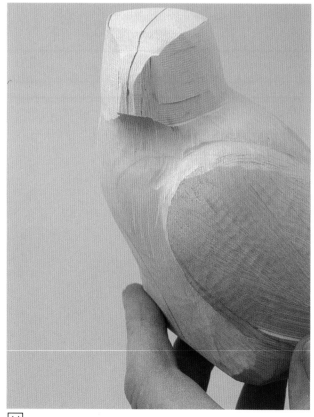

11 *The forehead is sloped down and the roughed-out bill is formed.*

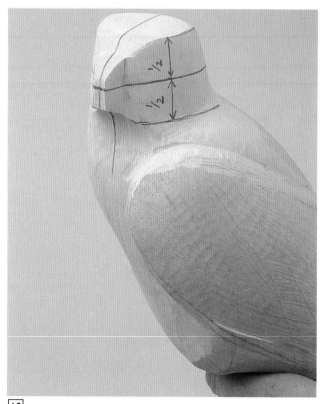

12 *Divide the profile of the head and draw a straight line from the front of the bill all the way around to the other side.*

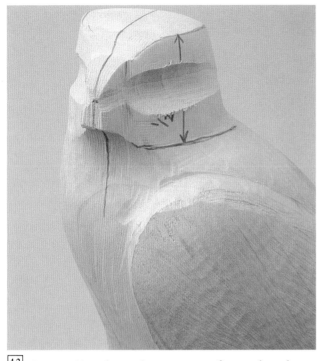

13 *Using a ⅜-inch round cutter, carve a furrow along the lines about ⅛ inch deep.*

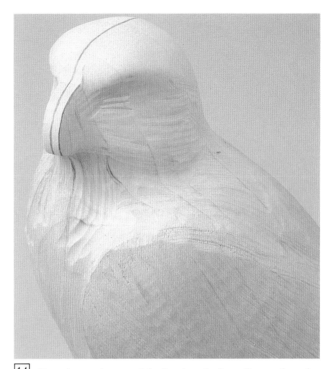

14 *Round over the top of the head to the brow line and sand smooth. With a ⅜-inch ruby stone, carve a channel just below the jaw line and round it off. At this point you can see the raptor like shape of the head beginning to form.*

15 *After studying and measuring your reference material, draw in the final bill and cere shape.*

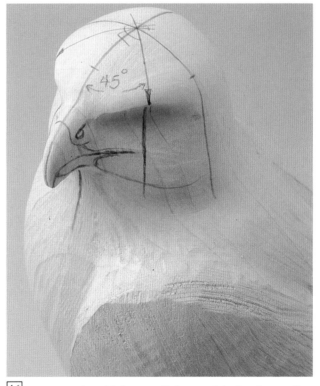

16 *Lay out a line 45 degrees off the top of the head center line and draw it straight down the side of the head and into the eye channel.*

17 *Absolute symmetry is essential when drawing these vertical lines in order to establish the correct eye layout. At this point, the final nostril placement can be drawn in.*

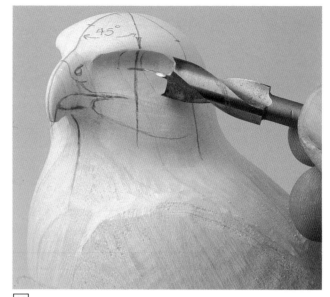

18 *The eye layout mark is located directly behind and in line with the nostril, approximately centered in the eye channel. The actual eye socket is initially drilled with a ⅜-inch spur bit or wood-boring bit.*

19 *Widen the eye sockets using a round ruby stone. This is necessary in order to enlarge the eye sockets under the brow ridge without disturbing the wood of the brow.*

20 *Refine the bill and carve in a slight ridge to separate the upper mandible from the lower. Ream out the nostril and establish a distinct line between bill and cere.*

21 The eyes are set in the sockets, embedded into a clay like mixture of two-part plumber's epoxy putty. A pencil eraser is a handy tool for pressing in and focusing the eyes. Take extra time and patience with this step.

22 My choice for eyelid material is A & B epoxy putty made by the Biggs Company of California and sold by Craft Cove of Illinois. It is rolled out like a thin snake and carefully laid around the perimeter of the eye.

23 Use sharpened toothpicks and a small palette knife to shape the eyelid. The putty begins to set in about an hour so you must work quickly.

24 The two eyes look remarkably different. A distinct raptor-like look is achieved once the eyelid is in place, which is why this is one of my favorite stages in the sculpting process.

25 Once the bill is shaped and sanded with 600-grit wet or dry sandpaper, the entire bill and cere are soaked with Super Glue, creating a very hard, resilient surface.

26 After the directional feather flow is penciled in, it's time for the final texturing.

Making Eyes

THERE COMES A POINT IN THE DEVELOPMENT OF AN artist's abilities and techniques when he must push the limits of the art form, searching for innovation—not for its own sake, but to further express the passion he feels for the art. With luck he will create something new, fresh, and exciting. This is the mark of a true artist. Every now and then someone comes up with a new twist, something done a little differently, that redirects the focus of the art. In the early 1980s, Eldridge Arnold of Connecticut used geometric shapes on which to present his bird carvings. He reasoned that by emphasizing the bird as the focal point and simplifying its surroundings he could make a stronger statement compositionally, thereby allowing the essence of the bird to emerge unhindered. As he put it, "I was tired of dirt and wanted to get my birds out of the salad bowl." He was reacting to the popular trend at the time of including lots of fabricated flora and fauna from the bird's habitat, creating a miniature natural history diorama. Arnold's new approach caught on quickly and was further developed and perfected by other great artists, most notably by Larry Barth's 1986 portrayal of a pair of common terns in flight. Other innovations were to quickly follow.

For those of us who specialize in sculpting birds of prey, a real problem has always been finding glass eyes that have that convincing "spark of life," the intensity needed to portray the essence of a predatory bird. The variety of colors, patterns, and pupil sizes of raptors' eyes just couldn't accurately be replicated by the few companies manufacturing glass eyes for taxidermists and bird sculptors. Greg Woodard, a falconer and world champion carver from Utah, solved this dilemma by developing a way to fabricate his own eyes for his many raptor carvings, thus giving them an additional look of realism and injecting into each bird its own personality. Inspired by Greg's ideas, I began experimenting in 1990 with ways of making eyes for my own raptor carvings. My first attempt was with a red-tailed hawk sculpture called "Windigo." The better part of three months was spent perfecting this technique, and after much trial and error, it now seems to work quite well for me.

The following sequence shows how I fabricate eyes using a few easily obtainable materials.

1 *Acrylic sheet can be purchased in various thicknesses but I recommend using no width thicker than ½ inch.*

2 *First wash the surface with warm soapy water to remove any chemical residue left over from the manufacturing process. A clean dry surface allows the paint to flow from the brush tip and form an absolutely perfect dot. Choose a paint color of carbon black to which a bit of flow medium has been added.*

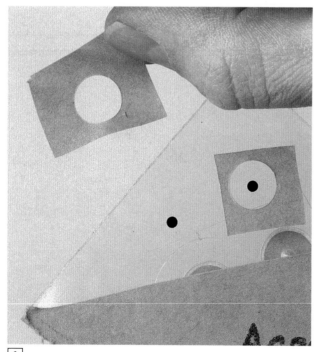

3 *From brown paper with adhesive backing, cut out circles slightly larger than the final eye diameter. Place the circles over the black pupils.*

4 *Once the paper cutouts are perfectly centered over the pupils, you are ready for the painting process.*

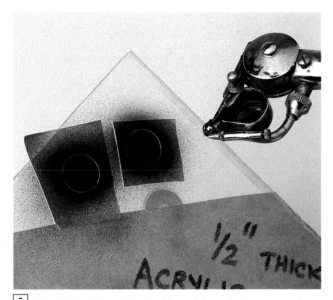

5 An airbrush is an invaluable tool for painting an eye. It enables the artist to blend colors subtly and achieve delicate shading. Unlike painting a feather, when the sequence is to paint from light to dark, the artist must think in reverse when painting an eye and paint the darkest colors first.

6 After the final eye color has been achieved, iridescent white is thickly applied over the painted surface. I find this helps to brighten the eye by reflecting light back through the layers of paint. Remember to allow each successive layer of paint to dry thoroughly before applying another coat.

7 Once the iridescent paint has dried, apply pure white gesso over the entire surface.

8 The completely primed and painted eye.

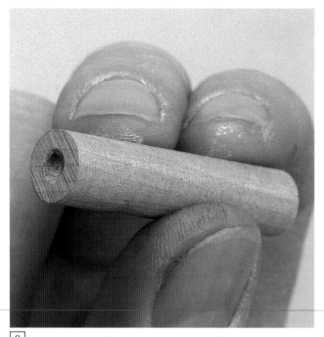

9 *Birch hardwood dowels are cut to 2 inches in length and a slight depression is ground into one end to allow clearance for the slightly elevated pupil.*

10 *Use Devcon 5-minute epoxy, center the dowels over eyes, and glue them into place.*

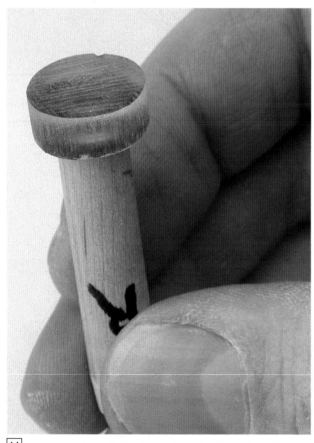

11 *Bandsaw the individual eyes from the sheet of acrylic. They now look like plastic discs.*

12 *A ⅜-inch stump cutter works well to shape the plastic. Be sure to wear eye protection when carving the acrylic as it is very hard and particles fly everywhere.*

13 *The final shape is achieved. Now you are ready to sand.*

14 *Mount the eye upside down in a drill press and sand and shape it with 150-grit sandpaper until all of the carving marks are eliminated.*

15 *The final sanding is done with 600-grit sandpaper.*

16 *Use a jeweler's cotton wheel and rouge to polish the convex surface of the eye and remove any small scratches or imperfections.*

17 *Holding the eye up to a light for close inspection, you will be able to see any imperfections that should be buffed out.*

18 *Cut off the birch dowel, leaving approximately a ⅛-inch stump on the back of the eye. The eye is now ready to be set into the eye socket and finished.*

Gallery

"Integrity"
American bald eagle, 1991
Collection of Dick and Barbara Weinand,
Coventry, Rhode Island
Tupelo and acrylics

An adult female bald eagle strikes a dramatic up-right pose as it flares its massive wings. Perched on a dead snag along an Alaskan river bank, our national bird prepares to settle down after gorging on spawning salmon.

Just the burning of each of the individual feathers on the body and wings took up the better part of a month. I had to overcome certain technical problems in order to shape such a massive piece of wood into an eagle. An electric chain saw was specially modified for removing large volumes of wood rapidly. The teeth were filed almost 90 degrees to the bar to prevent the saw from digging into the block too quickly. As the form was refined, auto-body sanders were used to block in the major muscle and feather groups. The body and tail are one block of wood, and each wing was carved from a separate block. No inserts were used because I wanted to take a more sculptural approach and carve volume into the wings. A common problem with inserts is that they tend to *look* inserted and thus lack the flow and rhythm of the real feather groups.

Knowing what type of texturing to do to achieve certain effects comes only with experience. As a general rule, I usually stone soft-edged or white feathers and rely on my burning pen to texture the hard-edged or major flight feathers. I followed this rule while texturing this bald eagle. The head and neck areas (all the white feathers) have been textured only with a small white cylinder, while the remaining brown contour and major flight feathers were burned.

Five and a half months of very intense work were required to see this sculpture through to completion.

"Windigo"
Eastern red-tailed hawk, 1990
Collection of Dr. and Mrs. Myron Yanoff,
Philadelphia, Pennsylvania
Tupelo, basswood, and acrylics

It was snowing lightly that day in mid–February 1988 as a friend and I were riding up the chairlift of a local ski area. Approaching the top of the mountain, we swayed in the wind several hundred feet above the ground, suspended by an inch and a half of steel cable. About 150 feet to our right, the remains of an old elm tree jutted out from the side of a cliff, a blowdown of long ago wedged between two giant crags in the rock wall. I wasn't the only one who noticed this stark, silvery snag—a red-tailed hawk swept up past us and alighted on one of the outermost branches. As soon as the raptor grabbed onto its perch, a gust of wind caught it off balance. The disoriented hawk struggled against the wind to regain its balance, with each blast flaring its rufous tail and flashing its silvery underwings. This display reminded me of the flamenco dancers of Spain dancing, twirling, flaring up their billowing dresses to the beat of the castañuelas.

This scene lasted only five seconds but the visual impact excited me as the composition began to come together in my mind. The next day I began working up sketches of basic geometric shapes to convey animation. Then I put away my sketchbook for about a year before I began work on a red-tailed hawk commission and rekindled that creative fire.

The branch, carved of basswood, flows down onto the black lacquered base to clutch it with raptorlike talons. The base itself is multifaceted to reflect light, which gives a visual impression of wind blowing from below and billowing out certain feather groups on the hawk. The weight and center of gravity are placed directly over the right foot as the left foot lightly touches the upper section of the branch. The wide-eyed intensity, flared nape feathers, and partially opened mouth portray the displeasure this bird is feeling at this particular moment.

I named this piece in honor of a nesting pair of red-tailed hawks that live just off the driveway close to our house. Each year they raise their young in full view of all who come to visit us at *Windigo*.

"A Question of Balance"
Arctic gyrfalcon and Atlantic puffin, 1987
Collection of Andy and Sandy Andrews, Jackson,
Michigan
Tupelo and acrylics

The predator-prey relationship is one that has always fascinated me. It's amazing how some creatures have evolved to overcome and kill, while others have developed defensive and evasive traits to prevent being eaten. The whole process is sort of like a natural history arms race: one side develops a new weapon and the other side develops a defense to counter the threat.

Gyrfalcons come well equipped to survive their harsh environment. Large and powerful, perfectly colored and fast on the wing, they feed on a variety of arctic creatures including seabirds. In this sculpture an Atlantic puffin crossed the path of a hungry gyrfalcon and after a brief pursuit was caught and brought up to a rock ledge. The strong diagonal lines of the rocks denote motion as they project downward at an angle exactly opposite that of the falcon's body. The dead puffin is in a submissive pose, flopped over the rock, yet even in death it is defiant, as evidenced by the foot of the puffin still pushing against the belly of the falcon.

Color was one factor in choosing the prey species. Atlantic puffins grow brightly colored horns over their bills and around their eyes during breeding season. The brilliant yellow coloring in the bill works well with the pale yellow cere and feet of the gyrfalcon, while the stark white breast and jet black back of the puffin and the white and black patterns of the large falcon create a visual counterpoint.

"Fragile Sovereignty"
Adult golden eagle, 1989
Collection of Dr. and Mrs. Myron Yanoff,
Philadelphia, Pennsylvania
Tupelo, birch plywood, and acrylics

One of the most formidable creatures to take wing, the golden eagle reigns supreme over all it surveys. Such at least was the case before *Homo sapiens* entered the picture and began shooting, uprooting, and polluting the fragile ecosystem these great birds once ruled.

In designing this sculpture, I sought to create a portrait of an incredibly powerful, well-designed killing machine; a large, magnificent collection of muscles, feathers, rapierlike talons, and keen eyes thought by many ornithologists to be the most highly evolved of all the bird species; so totally in control . . . yet so helplessly vulnerable to mankind's destructive whims.

The large black pyramid is representative of the lofty mountains where these birds nest. Balancing precariously atop is a long rock teetering on a fulcrum point, signifying the delicate balance of nature, a balance that must be maintained if our world is to survive. Whether we live in cities, small towns, or the deep woods, as the eagles disappear and the species becomes a memory, we can't be far behind.

With the exception of the right wing, the entire eagle is carved from one block of tupelo wood. The carving and painting took some twelve hundred hours of studio time over a period of seven months to complete.

"Counterstrike!"

Eastern red-tailed hawk and copperhead snake, 1992
Collection of Roger Jones, Falls Church, Virginia
Tupelo and acrylics

The age-old struggle for survival is played out in this highly animated sculpture depicting two formidable predators. The red-tailed hawk is one of the most adaptable and successful large raptors in North America, due in part to the wide range of prey in its diet. One of the few predatory birds that will eat even toads, red-tails often feed on a variety of reptiles, including venomous snakes such as the copperhead depicted here.

In an effort to add tension and drama, I chose a copperhead snake as the prey because of its potentially lethal attributes. In addition, the light-phase southeastern copperhead's cryptic patterning and rich copper coloring nicely balance the hawk's deep browns and rusts.

While researching snakes for this piece, I learned that up to three hours after a snake dies its nervous system still causes the tail to twitch. I wanted to convey a sense of movement throughout the entire composition. I borrowed an old cartoonist's trick of drawing in several forms to illustrate motion, which accounts for the additional tails carved into the base.

The bird, the snake, and the base/branch were each sculpted from one block of wood. The feelings of force, flow, and unity were the overriding factors guiding me through this rather complicated work that spanned the better part of five months. Extra care was taken in detailing subtle areas such as the inside of the mouth and the white, scaly flaking on the talons. Note the drop of saliva on the tongue.

"Life in the Fast Lane"
Sharp-shinned hawk, 1993
Collection of Norman and Carole Leckert
Bethel, Vermont
Tupelo and acrylics

Compositionally I wanted to convey the pent-up energy and electric personality of the sharp-shinned hawk. Its steel blue coloring and sleek lines combine to create a bird of elegance both on the wing and when perched. To be sure, if you blinked your eye or looked away for a split second it would be gone.

This hungry female sharpie has just nailed a cedar waxwing. I chose the cedar waxwing feeling that its appropriate size would balance nicely with the small size of the sharp-shin.

Cedar waxwings, being swift on the wing, don't succumb easily to predators, even the fleet sharp-shinned hawk. The position of the prey in this story of life and death is critical as the waxy red tips of the cedar waxwing's secondary feathers work nicely against the red eyes of the hunter. This also creates a non-graphic interpretation of the blood that would most certainly be involved in such a scene.

"The Vigil"
American kestrel, 1992
Collection of Dr. Gloria Young, Pennsylvania
Tupelo, basswood, and acrylics

When an idea or design is used more than once in a painting or sculpture it is known as a repetition of theme. This can take many forms, from subtle splashes of the same color to the duplication of an actual shape, as is the case in this portrait of a lone American kestrel.

The dynamics of the carved rocks seem to enhance the defiant personality of this little hunter. Of the many physical characteristics unique to the diurnal raptors, one of the most striking is the triangular shape of the top of the head. In designing this composition, I made a pattern of the top of the kestrel's head and enlarged it many times to achieve the desired shape of the rock. The large, flat, sloping surface seems like a giant shadow cast by this little juggernaut.

The bird itself puts forth an air of self-assurance as it scans the skies, daring anything to enter its territory. During breeding season kestrels are notoriously territorial and will exhibit extremely aggressive behavior in driving off anything that flies nearby. It is certainly not uncommon to observe a pair of kestrels dive-bombing and harassing a hawk, owl, or even an eagle until the confused intruder exits the invisible boundary of the kestrels' territory.

"Caught on the Wing"
American kestrel and dragonfly, 1993
Collection of Alan and Chris Reiman, Merced, California
Tupelo, acrylics, and cellophane

Few creatures possess the amazing powers of flight bestowed upon the dragonfly. It can fly at tremendous speed yet stop instantly; it can even fly backward and sideways! Despite this aerial prowess, when a hungry kestrel is patrolling the area, even a dragonfly must beware.

Kestrels can often be seen darting about over meadows snatching grasshoppers, flies, dragonflies, and small birds, eating on the wing until their hunger is satiated.

I refer to this composition as an honest way of telling a story of predator and prey. Instead of a cute little field mouse or chickadee as the victim, which might cause the viewer to feel sorrow, I chose a dragonfly, whose mechanical, almost robotic look seems to draw little sympathy. As a result one is able to focus on the kestrel and applaud its flying and hunting proficiency.

Bibliography

The following is a list of the invaluable references used during the preparation of this book.

Books:

Beebe, Frank L. *Hawks, Falcons and Falconry.* Blaine, WA: Hancock House Publishers, 1987.

Bent, Arthur Cleveland. *Life Histories of North American Birds of Prey,* 2 vols. New York: Dover Publications, Inc., 1961.

Blanchan, Neltje. *Birds That Hunt and Are Hunted.* New York: Doubleday & McClure Co., 1898.

Brooke, Michael and Birkhead, Tim. *The Cambridge Encyclopedia of Ornithology.* Cambridge, England: Cambridge University Press, 1991.

Brown, Leslie and Amadon, Dean. *Eagles, Hawks and Falcons of the World.* Secaucus, NJ: The Wellfleet Press, 1968.

Bruce, David. *Bird of Jove.* New York: Ballantine Books, 1971.

Bull, John and Farrand, John Jr. *The Audubon Society Field Guide to North American Birds: Eastern Region.* New York: Alfred A. Knopf, 1977.

Cade, Tom J. *The Falcons of the World.* Ithaca, NY: Cornell University Press, 1982.

Craighead, John J. and Craighead, Frank C. Jr. *Hawks, Owls, and Other Wildlife.* New York: Dover Publications, Inc., 1969.

Gerrard, Jon M. and Bortolotti, Gary R. *The Bald Eagle: Haunts and Habits of a Wilderness Monarch.* Washington: Smithsonian Institution Press, 1988.

Grossman, Mary Louise and Hamlet, John. *Birds of Prey of the World.* New York: Clarkson N. Potter, Inc., 1964.

Hosking, Eric; Hosking, David; and Flegg, Jim. *Birds of Prey of the World.* Lexington, MA: The Stephen Greene Press, 1987.

Johnsgard, Paul A. *Hawks, Eagles, and Falcons of North America.* Washington: Smithsonian Institution Press, 1990.

Leeson, Tom and Leeson, Pat. *The American Eagle.* Hillsboro, OR: Beyond Words Publishing, 1988.

Mackenzie, John P. *Birds of the World.* Ashland, WI: Paper Birch Press, Inc., 1986. Vol. 1: *Birds of Prey.*

Newton, Ian. *Population Ecology of Raptors.* Vermillion, SD: Buteo Books, 1979.

Page, Jake and Morton, Eugene S. *Lords of the Air.* Washington: Smithsonian Books, 1989.

Palmer, Ralph S. *Handbook of North American Birds,* vols. 4 and 5. New Haven, CT: Yale University Press, 1988.

Peterson, Roger Tory. *A Field Guide to the Birds.* Boston: Houghton Mifflin Co., 1980.
Ratcliffe, Derek. *The Peregrine Falcon.* Vermillion, SD: Buteo Books, 1980.

Reader's Digest Editors. *Reader's Digest Book of North American Birds.* New York: Reader's Digest Association, Inc., 1990.

Savage, Candace. *Eagles of North America.* Ashland, WI: North Word, Inc., 1987.

Snyder, Noel and Snyder, Helen. *Birds of Prey: Natural History and Conservation of North American Raptors.* Stillwater, MN: Voyageur Press, Inc., 1991.

Sprunt, Alexander Jr. *North American Birds of Prey.* New York: Harper & Bros., 1955.

Terres, John K. *The Audubon Society Encyclopedia of North American Birds.* New York: Alfred A. Knopf, 1980.

Wetmore, Alexander. *Water, Prey and Game Birds of North America.* Washington: National Geographic Society, 1965.

Periodicals:

American Birds Magazine. 700 Broadway, New York, NY 10003.

Audubon Magazine. 700 Broadway, New York, NY 10003.

Birder's World Magazine. 44 E. 8th Street, Suite 410, Holland, MI 49423.

Breakthrough Magazine. P.O. Box 1320, Loganville, GA 30249.

The Living Bird Quarterly. Laboratory of Ornithology at Cornell University, 159 Sapsucker Woods Road, Ithaca, NY 14850.

Wildbird Magazine. P.O. Box 6050, Mission Viejo, CA 92690.

Wildfowl Art. Journal of the Ward Foundation, 655 S. Salisbury Boulevard, Salisbury, MD 21801.

Wildfowl Carving and Collecting Magazine. Box 1831, Harrisburg, PA 17105.

Wildlife Art News. P.O. Box 16246, Minneapolis, MN 55416.